Wisdom Nuggets

CHIDINMA

Kingdom Publishers

Wisdom Nuggets
Copyright © Chidinma

All rights reserved. No part of this book may be reproduced in any form by photocopying or any electronic or mechanical means, including information storage or retrieval systems, without permission in writing from both the copyright owner and the publisher of the book. The right of Chidinma to be identified as the author of this work has been asserted by her in accordance with the Copyright, Designs and Patents Act 1988 and any subsequent amendments thereto.
A catalogue record for this book is available from the British Library.

All Scripture Quotations have been taken from the New International Version and the King James Version of the Bible.

ISBN: 978-1-913247-78-2

1st Edition by Kingdom Publishers
Kingdom Publishers
London, UK.

You can purchase copies of this book from any leading bookstore or email **contact@kingdompublishers.co.uk**

DEDICATION

This book is dedicated to The Holy Spirit, my Teacher.

CHAPTER 1

Nugget 1
Share Jesus

Nugget 2
Remember Not The Former Things

Nugget 3
God Can Do It Again

Nugget 4
Pay What You Have Vowed To God

Nugget 5
Jesus Is The Door

Nugget 6
God's Strength Is Made Perfect In Weakness

Nugget 7
God Thinks About You

Nugget 8
Be Led By The Spirit Of God Not By Flesh

Nugget 9
Blessed Is He That Believes

Nugget 10
Blessed Is The Man That Fears The Lord

NUGGET 1 - Share Jesus

Bible Reading: **Luke 2: 11**
For unto you is born this day in the city of David a Savior, which is Christ the Lord.

Christmas and Easter periods are usually times we celebrate the birth of Jesus, His death and His resurrection. He loved us so much that He left His abode in heaven, came down to earth and died on the cross for our sins. So amid the presents, decorations, cookings and parties, please remember the reason for the birth of Jesus Christ and His death and the significance of these celebrations to everyone who believes.

We know that these are seasons to share gifts and as we arrange to share our gifts, let us think of the best gift ever to share which is the gift of Christ and His love for mankind. Let us share the gift of Jesus to those who have not known Him nor the power of His resurrection.

Share Christ to those who do not know that they need Him in their lives because there are so many people who do not know who Jesus is and who do not even know the reasons for Christmas and Easter celebrations. Many people do not know that this same Jesus that was born to save mankind will be coming back again for those who are saved.

Beloved we need to use these seasons to tell the world about Christ and His kingdom and always include in our gift packages, Christian books, pamphlets and bibles to help promote the knowledge of Christ.

NUGGET 2 - Remember Not The Former Things

Bible Reading: **Isaiah 43:18**
Remember ye not the former things, neither consider the things of old.

Beloved as each day, week or year ends and the Lord graciously ushers us into a new one, let us try as much as we can not to enter the new with the bitterness, sorrows, disappointments and failures of the previous times. Let us lay aside every sin and weights that easily beset us and not remember the hurts, the unforgiveness and the pains of yesteryears. Let us not carry over any hate or revenge or ill actions of the previous times into this brand new one.

The scripture above enjoined us to remember not the former things, the former ways, the former bad experiences and the former bad behaviours. The scripture did not end there; it continued that we should not consider the things of the old at all for old things are passed away and all things have become new.

The previous times may have been tough and rough with so many unachieved dreams and unanswered prayers but as we have been given the grace to see a brand new day/week/year we should endeavor to enter with a new faith and hope that all will be well. Let us not have the mindset that this present time might also be like the previous.

This is a new day, week, month or year, drop the old and begin the new. Tell God to do a new thing in your life, in your family, in your business, in your career, in your walk and in your relationship with Him and in any other area that requires a new touch from God and that God that does new things will visit you according to your heart desires.

NUGGET 3 - God Can Do It Again

Bible Reading: **1st Samuel 17:37**
David said moreover, the Lord that delivered me out of the paw of the lion, and out of the paw of the bear, He will deliver me out of the hand of this Philistine. And Saul said unto David, go and the Lord be with thee.

Beloved, God is good Himself and can never cease in doing good. He is good all the time. God never changes, there is no shadow of turning with Him. Has He done anything good for you before, He will do it again and He is very well able to do that which He has done for you before and over again.

In the above scripture, David was faced with a difficult situation of defeating a great warrior from Philistine who had won several battles for his people. David remembered that God had helped him before on several occasions. With the confidence that that same God who helped him before will still do it again, he was able to remove fear and conquer the enemy despite the fact that the enemy involved was a very dreadful one.

That God of David is still the same God we serve now, He has not changed and there is no situation on earth that anyone is facing now that has never been handled by God before and He is still in the business of handling issues and can handle any issue we present to Him. So beloved, as you begin a new day, if there are still some unanswered prayers please remember all that He has done for you before, just like David did and be confident that He will still do it again.

NUGGET 4 - Pay What You Have Vowed To God

Bible Reading: **Ecclesiastes 5:4**
When thou vowest a vow unto God, defer not to pay it; for He has no pleasure in fools. Pay that which thou hast vowed.

A vow is a promise and a vow made to God is a promise made to God. When you make a vow before God, it is self imposed law that you must keep. If you do not keep the vow, you have committed a sin against God because you have made a promise to God you did not keep it. It is a good thing to make a vow before God because in so doing you set spiritual goals for yourself which will in turn bring glory to God and attract God's blessings to you.

It is therefore worthy to note that when you make a vow before God's representative then you must keep the vow. Unfulfilled vows attract God's anger. Making promises to God and not keeping them is a mockery to Him and God cannot be mocked.

Beloved have you made a vow to God at any point in your life? Have you at anytime promised God that if He does so so and so for you, you will do so so and so for Him? Have you made a promise to serve God for the rest of your life if He answers your prayers? Have you at anytime made a pledge before any of God's representatives? The vow could be money, time or others and you have not redeemed the vow, let this serve as a reminder for you to pay whatever vow you have made to God so that you will not hinder the maximum flow of God's blessings in your life.

NUGGET 5 - Jesus Is The Door...

Bible Reading: John 10:9
I am the door: by me if any man enters in, he shall be saved, and shall go in and out, and find pasture.

John 10:1 -9; 3:16, Acts 4:12, John 3:17

Jesus in the above scripture described Himself metaphorically as the door; the door to salvation. A door provides a means of access. Jesus is the door and through Him we both have access by the Spirit to the Father. He is the way, the truth and the life and no one comes to the Father except through Him. He is the door through which all must enter into the sheepfold of God. Beloved, Jesus is the door to your breakthrough; He is the door to your healing; He is the door to your wealth and any other good things that your heart desires. There is no other way except Him.

For you to go into a house, you must pass through the door. The door of your house gives you access to go into your house to relax, eat or drink and sleep. Not only does your door gives you access to your inner chambers it also gives your visitors same access to you or to go in and do anything authorized by you. Some unauthorized visitors go through the window to steal and no visitor of yours that you authorized to come into your house goes through the window. They must go through the door otherwise they will not be allowed to come in.

Beloved, Jesus is the right and the only way to access your heavenly father and the only way to heaven. We cannot claim to be candidates of heaven and still go to other gods in secret. We cannot call the name of God and call the name of Baal at the same time. We cannot serve God and serve mammon.

If we need money, we must go through the right door which is making sure our businesses and business dealings are clean. In everything we do, we must strive to do the right thing and go through the normal processes.

The scriptures is also showing us that there is no other name by which we can be saved but by the name of Jesus and there is no other that can bless us truly but Jesus. There is no restrictions with Jesus who is described as the door, you can go in and go out anytime you desire which means you can access Him anytime at all and from anywhere. He is always open for you even to find pastures.

NUGGET 6 - God's Strength Is Made Perfect In Weakness

Bible Reading: **2nd Corinthians 12:9**
And He said unto me, my grace is sufficient for thee: for my strength is made perfect in weakness. Most gladly therefore will I rather glory in my infirmities, that the power of Christ may rest upon me.

Judges 6:15, Job 4:3, Isaiah 40:29, Joel 3:10

Beloved, we are all flesh and blood and have one weakness or the other, one infirmity or the other just like Apostle Paul who was a faithful follower of Jesus Christ but with a thorn in his flesh. When he prayed to be released from his weakness, he received this answer: "My grace is sufficient for you, for my strength is made perfect in weakness."

The above statement concerns the grace of God's sufficiency to deal with all aspects of our lives. God is able to deliver us from this physical world. God is able to deliver us from sin and death. Therefore whether in the midst of physical sufferings, hardships, weaknesses and infirmities or in the midst of spiritual sufferings, we must trust that God is able to deliver us from them all. Such trust in God's grace will carry us through those hard times.

Apostle Paul learnt to trust in God's power to deliver. He did not trust in his strength, abilities, cleverness, or accomplishments to deal with his weaknesses and infirmity but he prayed to God and even when he got the type of answer he got from God, he still trusted Him. His weakness and infirmity glorified the name of Christ. When his weakness and infirmity were manifested, the power of God also manifested because it was through the power of Christ he was delivered. He was strong because the infirmity and hardship drove him to trust in God and not himself.

Apostle Paul was aware of his weakness and he received grace to deal with it in a way that glorified Christ. If you are aware of your weaknesses, be humble and go to God in prayer then receive grace to become strong in God, for His strength is made perfect in weakness. But then you will also flee from those things and from company that draws you to those weaknesses and you will pursue righteousness, faith, love, and peace with all those who call on the Lord out of a pure heart.

NUGGET 7 - God Thinks About You

Bible Reading: **Jeremiah 29: 11**
For I know the thoughts that I think towards you, saith the Lord, thoughts of peace, and not of evil, to give you an expected end.

Psalm 8:4, 2 Thessalonians 3:16, Psalm37:37

Beloved, do you know that if you are God's, He thinks about you all the time? His mind is always on you, His eyes too are always fixed on you 24 hours daily and He loves you so dearly and that love is everlasting.

Jeremiah 29:11 describes the kind of thoughts God thinks towards you. It says thoughts of peace and if God is thinking thoughts of peace for you, He will never allow the opposite to come near you even when trouble comes. God is so much committed to that thought that He thinks towards you so much that He will always device a means to give you that peace He has in mind for you no matter the magnitude of the wars you are fighting and no matter the potencies of the powers organizing the wars against you.

The scripture also says that His thoughts for you are not of evil which means that He thinks thoughts of good for you. And it does not matter who is thinking evil for you secretly or openly, God's thoughts will always overrule. It does not also matter what the devil, the evil master and planner is planning, God's good plans and thoughts will always prevail against his.

Finally the scripture says that God's thought and plan for you is to give you an expected end. Beloved what are you expecting this year end and beyond, the God whom you are His is giving you an expected end which is everything good that your heart desires.

NUGGET 8 - Be Led By The Spirit Of God Not By Flesh

Bible Reading: **Romans 8:14**
For as many as are led by the spirit of God, they are the sons of God.

Isaiah 30:21, Psalm 23:2 -3, John 10:3

God is a spirit and they that worship Him must worship Him in spirit and in truth and as many as are led by the spirit of God, they are the true sons of God.

Beloved, Romans 8:14 simply means that a true child of God receives directions from God and not from fleshy emotions. This also means that a true child of God is submitted to the will of God and seeks the will of God in order to determine the direction of his or her life and all that He or she does or says. On the other hand, those who are led by the flesh, follows after their flesh which leads them away from dependence on God for directions and everything they do or say revolves around the flesh and are completely out of God's will and directions.

Beloved since you are in Christ and a child of God, allow the spirit of God in you to lead you in all things; depend on Him for directions, and guidance while submitting to Him totally and wholeheartedly so that you will not give room to the flesh which yields no profit.

NUGGET 9 - Blessed Is She/He That Believes

Bible Reading: **Luke 1:45**
And blessed is she that believed: for there shall be a performance of those things which were told her from the Lord.

Mark 9:23
Jesus said unto him, if thou canst believe, all things are possible to him that believeth.

Mark 11:23-24, Mathew 9:29, Mathew 21:21

The first scripture said that there shall be a performance of those things. This means that those things that have been promised to us by the Father shall be done and the second scripture was a word from Jesus himself to a fellow man like you and I saying that everything is possible only if we would believe.

Beloved, that same Jesus is still speaking to us today that only if we can believe, only if we can trust and only if we can have faith in Him that every good thing we desire shall be ours. This means that that contract you have been desiring to get is possible, the completion of that house is possible, that healing of your body is possible, the salvation or the repentance of that your loved one you have been praying for is possible; that position you have been desiring and asking God for is possible.

Beloved, just everything is possible only if you believe and remember it will not cost you anything to believe but it will cost you your heart desires if you do not believe. Choose to believe God today and you shall be blessed with all that your heart desires for blessed is he that believes and there shall be a performance of all those things that God has promised.

NUGGET 10 - Blessed Is The Man That Fears The Lord

Bible Reading: **Psalms 128:1-2**
Blessed is every one that feareth the Lord; that walketh in His ways. For thou shalt eat the labour of thine hands: happy shalt thou be and it shall be well with thee.

Job 28:28, Psalm 2: 11; 15:4; 34:7&9; 89:7, P roverbs 9:10

The Psalmist enumerated some of the benefits you will receive from the Lord if you fear Him and walk in His ways. The Lord is a rewarder; He rewards every action of man towards Him; He is a paymaster, you can never work for Him in vain and He rewards both here on earth and hereafter.

According by the scriptures, if you fear the Lord and walk in His ways, you shall be blessed, you shall eat the labour of thine hands, you shall be happy and it shall be well with you. Beloved what more can one ask for. Please note that you cannot fear the Lord and not obey His commands. You must walk in His ways; you must please Him. Fearing the Lord comes from knowing the Lord and knowing the Lord comes from studying His words and

and studying His words, obeying and applying them to your daily life brings good success to all aspects of your life (Joshua 1:8).

CHAPTER 2

Nugget 11
Neither Do I Condemn You, Go And Sin No More

Nugget 12
Grace Is All You Need

Nugget 13
In God's Time He Makes All Things Beautiful

Nugget 14
Bask Yourself In The Holy Ghost
And You Would Not Have Time For Sin

Nugget 15
They That Be With Us Are More

Nugget 16
Acquaint Thyself With The Lord

Nugget 17
Be Of Good Cheer!

Nugget 18
If God Be For Us...

Nugget 19
Repay No Man Evil For Evil

Nugget 20
Fight The Good Fight Of Faith

NUGGET 11 - Neither Do I Condemn You, Go And Sin No More

Bible Reading: **John 8: 11**
She said, no man Lord. And Jesus said unto her, neither do I condemn thee: go and sin no more.

Isaiah 1:18; 43:25, Psalms 19:13, Romans 6:1 -2, 1John 3:9

The Scribes and Pharisees brought a woman who was caught in the very act of adultery to Jesus and quoted a law that said she should be stoned to death but Jesus instantly forgave her and asked her to go and sin no more.

This act of Jesus in this case simply tells us that Jesus can forgive you your sins and count them as past but He expects you not to continue in sin.

In Romans 6:1-2, Apostle Paul asked -shall we continue to sin so that grace may abound? And he answered and said in the next verse, God forbid! How can we claim to be dead in sin and still continue to live in sin. This means that it is forbidden for us to continue to sin and say in our hearts that God is merciful and therefore will forgive. It is very important to remember that God is also a consuming fire. It is true that the blood of Jesus cleanses us from all sins but it is also true that Jesus expects us to go and sin no more.

Beloved presumptuous sin is very dangerous, you might never know how God will reward it so let us be careful and pray like the Psalmist in Psalms 19:13 and God will help us as we prayed.

NUGGET 12 - Grace Is All You Need

Bible Reading: **Romans 5:2**
By whom also we have access by faith into this grace wherein we stand, and rejoice in hope of the glory of God.

John 1:14&16, Romans 5:17;   11:16, Hebrew 12:15, James 4:6

Grace is an unmerited favour; a special favour not deserved. Many a times we wonder how a God so big could condescend so low to have time for us. It is simply because of His grace and because He loves us and even when we have not done enough for Him, He still chooses to bless us anyways. In the world today, there are some sorts of qualifications or criteria to get certain things in life but the grace of God can make you get those things with ease, without qualification or meeting the required criteria.

Beloved we need the grace of God in this present world full of favouritism and nepotism. Grace of God can get you that job they termed exclusively for the children of the rich and famous. Grace of God can give you that contract they said you must pay to get. Grace of God can get you that position they said you must lobby or compromise to get. Grace of God can take you to the zenith of your career without settlement to the authorities concerned as obtainable in some places today.

Beloved, it is the grace of God that makes miracles happen. Why do you think God answers your prayers? Because you deserve it? No! He answers our prayers because of grace and because He wants to. God works answers in our lives because He wants to and He works miracles just because He loves us.

God's grace is without boundaries and it is limitless but Hebrew 12:15 says that one of the things that limits God's grace in our lives is bitterness. When you get resentful and allow bitterness build up in your life towards another, it hinders the grace of God in your life. Another hinderance to God's grace in our lives is pride (James 4:6). God hates pride so much that He can resist everything you do if you happen to exhibit or have pride in your life.

So beloved let us do away with anything that will hinder

NUGGET 13 - In God's Time He Makes All Things Beautiful

Bible Reading: **Ecclesiastes 3: 11**
He hath made everything beautiful in His time: also He hath set the world in their heart, so that no man can find out the work that God maketh from the beginning to the end.

God is the one who rules in the affairs of men; He is the monarch of the whole universe. He is the creator of all things for His pleasure and glory and there is beauty in all that He had made and makes. God is the owner of times and everything He does is done in His own time. He does things in times He feels suitable enough. God upholds, governs and orders all things according to the counsel of His will. God does somethings immediately and some not immediately according to His will, purpose and plan because He is the wisest and all knowing God and He knows exactly when and how best. Whenever and whichever way He does things, there is always beauty and harmony in all that He does.

Beloved having known that God is a beautiful, wise and all knowing God who does beautiful things at His own time, I want you to also know that He will visit you at His own time. I want you to also know that no power, no human, nor demon can stop God when the time for Him to visit you is due and He decides to. In fact you will become one of the most dangerous persons on earth because God can do anything and can go to any length to do that which it is time for Him to do.

NUGGET 14 - Bask Yourself In The Holy Ghost And You Won't Have Time For Sin

Bible Reading: Galatians 5:16
This I say then, walk in the spirit, and ye shall not fulfil the lust of the flesh.

Mathew 24:22, Mark 14:38, John 1:13; 3:6; 6:63, Rom 8:1-13

Beloved, the Holy Spirit is the spirit of God; He is holy and cannot condone any unholiness in any form. The Holy Spirit has been given to us as a check. He checks us against sin and against wrongdoing. He cannot behold iniquity, that is why the bible says that whosoever that is a carrier of the Holy Spirit should depart from iniquity. You cannot carry the Holy Spirit and sin at the same time though there are times we may fall as humans but it is quite different from having to sin routinely and having sin as part of you.

Constant and deliberate act of sin cannot be tolerated by the Holy Spirit. Holy Spirit is a spirit that moves where righteousness thrives and abounds. Once a person accepts Christ and gets born again, the Holy Spirit is expected to dwell in such a person to direct and to guide unto righteousness. He is the one that disturbs your heart and makes you uncomfortable when you accidentally falls into sin but when you make sin a habit and you do not see anything wrong with it, the Holy Spirit instantly moves away because the environment is no longer conducive for Him to stay and such a christian becomes an empty vessel and every action of such a person becomes fleshy and earthy.

According to Apostle Paul in Galatians 5:16, if you walk in the spirit, you will not yield to flesh or lust or sin. In other words when the desire to sin comes the spirit of God in you will enable you not to fulfil that desire; He will help you overcome it. Walking in the spirit is living after the direction of the Holy Spirit which He gives through the word of God (Hebrews 4:12)

Beloved, you would not know how to behave in a godly manner if you do not have directions from the Holy Spirit and when you follow the inspired word of God, you will truly walk in the spirit and fulfilling the lust of the flesh becomes impossible for you. When you bask yourself in the Holy Ghost, walk in the Holy Ghost, move into the Holy Ghost, you will not have time for sin.

NUGGET 15 - In God's Time He Makes All Things Beautiful

Bible Reading: **2nd Kings 6:16**
And he answered, fear not: for they that be with us are more than they that be with them.

1 John 4:4

2nd Kings 6:16 were Prophet Elisha's words to his servant who became perplexed and overwhelmed at the sight of a host of army of Syria who came by night and compassed them.

Beloved, are the enemies of your destiny so many? Have those you have not done anything thing to and the powers that be vowed that you will never amount to anything no matter how hard you try? Has someone vowed to deal with you because they think they have what it takes to? Has anyone you have been so good to paid you back evil for your good? Has anyone gone to bear false witness and told lies against you before your helpers? Is anyone not happy that things are going well for you? Is anyone always happy when you are sad thereby trying everything within his power to keep you sad? Has anyone seen that his plans against you failed and now after your life? Are there situations that right now are too much for you to handle? Are there powers that have vowed that they will not let you rest until they destroyed your home, your business, your work and finances? Are there powerful powers sponsoring all kinds of evil in your life?

Beloved, know this fact that they that be with you are more than they that be with them just like Prophet Elisha. Also know that greater is He that is in you than He that is in them or whatever power they think they possess.

Relax, keep your cool, and fear not. All it will take is to focus on God alone and to develop a good personal relationship with Him for all power belongs to Him. When you develop that personal relationship with God, stay in that relationship, build it up, maintain it and treasure it with your whole heart. Do not ever loose it or trade it for any pleasure of sin then watch God open your eyes to see horses and chariots of fire fighting for you and you will hold your peace and actually know that they that be with you are more.

NUGGET 16 - Acquaint Thyself With The Lord

Bible Reading: **Job 22:21**
Acquaint now thyself with Him, and be at peace:
thereby good shall come unto thee.

To acquaint means to be familiar or conversant with something or someone. God is calling us today through the scriptures to be His acquaintances. God forbid that stones would be raised in our places to worship God. God so much desires a relationship with us because He loves us. He wants us closer to Him and to submit ourselves to Him. We can never loose anything by establishing that closer relationship with Him instead we gain a lot from His sweet gracious presence to unending miracles and obtaining mercies in times of needs. The word of God tells us that when we acquaint ourselves with Him we will find peace and goodness shall follow us all the days our lives.

Beloved, do you need peace in your inner man? Are you troubled on every side and are the situations around you such that gives you sleepless nights and much headaches? Do you want good to always look for you and come to you with so much ease? Then get yourselves closer to God; yield yourselves to the Holy Spirit who dwells in you and everything will be all right.

HOW CAN WE GET OURSELVES ACQUAINTED WITH GOD?

Search the scriptures and obey His words. If you are looking for Jesus, go to the Bible and you will find Him. If you want to get closer to Jesus, read His words daily, there you will find peace because His words give assurance and peace.

Pray without ceasing. Prayer simply means talking to God and you cannot claim to be someone's acquaintances without talking to that someone. 1st Thessalonians 5:17 says pray without ceasing which means talk to God always, continuously and without stopping.

Be friends with Jesus. Be intimate with Jesus to the extent that He can refer to you as a friend. He can tell you anything, even hidden things that ordinary eyes cannot see, things hidden from others. You will enjoy the privilege of knowing His mind and hearing directly from God the father. (John 15:15).

You will also be protected and good will pursue you all the days of your life. Jesus, your friend will always sieve all evils directed towards you and turn them to good before they get to you and you will be highly blessed and prosperous.

NUGGET 17 - Be Of Good Cheer!

Bible Reading: Acts 27:25
Wherefore, Sirs, be of good cheer: for I believe God, that it shall be even as it was told me.

Beloved, this is a word of encouragement for you, to be confident, courageous, bold and fearless even when you are faced with adversities or circumstances beyond your control. Apostle Paul was on a journey and at a point in his journey, there arose a fierce storm that threatened his life and that of those travelling with him. This life is a journey and at several points in this journey, you must encounter fierce storms threatening your destiny and existence just like Apostle Paul did and we must learn from him if we must sail through to safety and victory.

Apostle Paul told those traveling with him to be of good cheer. He was not perturbed or afraid of the storm as his fellow travelers were but he had courage, he was fearless and confident and relaxed even in the midst of the heavy storm because he knew what God had told him before the journey started that there shall be no loss.

Beloved, what has God told you? And it seems that your situation right now is trying to make God a liar. Consider what God has told you concerning that situation through His word. Just like Apostle Paul you have to relax, be confident, bold, courageous and fearless because of what God has said concerning that issue coupled with what God has personally ministered to you. God's word is able to make you relax even in the face of unpleasant events. The knowledge of the word of God gives peace in the face of adversity.

Apostle Paul believed God and trusted His words to him. He never doubted what God told him concerning that particular journey. Beloved, it is one thing to hear from God and another thing to believe Him for only those who believes are justified. Also remember that to him that believes, there shall be a performance of those things God has said. Beloved only believe, do not fear, do not doubt even when it is hard not to considering the circumstances.

Apostle Paul said "It shall be even as it was told me". He expressed his confidence in what was told him by God. It was not based on hearsay or mere words of men, but based on specific message from God. This teaches us to base our confidence in God and His words not on man or any other power. Once you have heard from God or from His word, believe that it shall be so and it shall be so.

Beloved, there is no need to be depressed, dejected, moody or sad because of that situation, be of good cheer; the Lord will see you through it all.

NUGGET 18 - If God Be For Us...

Bible Reading: **Romans 8:31**
What shall we now say to these things? If God be for us, who can be against us?

2nd Kings 6:16, John 4:4, Mathew 19:26

The devil and his agents including the sorrow, pains, suff erings, sins, guilt of sins, temptations, trials, all manner of sicknesses and diseases are all constantly against us, the beloved of Christ but God is for us. The scripture above reassures us that if God is for us, no body including the devil himself and all that he brings can ever be against us.

Beloved, do you know why He is for us; it is because He has freely given us His son to free us from sin and its guilt and condemnations. The Bible recorded that if He did not spare His own son but delivered Him up for us all to be crucified how can He then not freely give us all things. Also He has given us His Holy Spirit to guide us and His angels to guard us. He has chosen us and has made us His sons and daughters. He has brought us into His family and we can confidently call Him our father and we are by right entitled to enjoy all the benefits that comes from the adoption into His family and the fatherly protection that comes with it too. He has given us security here and eternal security hereafter.

Beloved, the moment we accept Christ into our hearts, Romans 8:31 automatically applies to us and our safety is guaranteed because the words in that scripture mean safety. It means that no harm can ever come our way and even if it comes, God will deliver us. If we have God. we have everything.

Therefore, if you are feeling insecure and having hard times in any area of your life, your option is to turn to God and His words. Remember what the scriptures said concerning your security. God's word in Psalms 118:6 says "the Lord is on my side, I will not fear: what can man do unto me?".

Relax, God is definitely for you and with you and If God be for you, what are you afraid of and who can be against you? NOBODY!

NUGGET 19 - Repay No Man Evil For Evil

Bible Reading: **Romans 12:17**
Recompense to no man evil for evil. Provide things honest in the sight of all men.

Mathew 6:12, Mark 11:26, Luke 17:4

The world is taught to revenge but as children of God we are not of the world, we are taught to behave and think differently from the rest of the world, to think and to act like our father. Christians are to repay evil with good, and the good christians do is not supposed to be dependent on the behaviour of others towards them but on what the scripture teaches and God's commands. The scripture teaches us to overcome evil with good.

We are to behave like our Heavenly Father who sends his rain on the good and on the evil. He makes the sun rise on the just and on the unjust. He sends his blessings on believers and unbelievers alike. He is good to everyone including His enemies, it does not matter if they believe in Him or not. Jesus our role model is a perfect example of not repaying evil for evil. While on the cross dying for our sins and the sins of those who crucified Him, He said "Father, forgive them; for they know not what they do...." He prayed for those who hurt Him even at the height of his pain and agony. Jesus' state of mind of forgiveness towards those who crucified Him should be same with ours when we face same situation.

Beloved, has anyone hurt you lately or in the past? Has any wrong or injustice been meted to you and you have vowed and planned to get even with whoever that was involved? No, that is not the right thing to do. The scriptures advised us not to repay that evil with evil. As children of God, we should not seek to get even with anyone who has wronged us but to leave the matter with God our father whom vengeance belongs to for He knows exactly what to do. It is not in our place to seek revenge. Do not be like those the scriptures referred to in Romans 3:8 that said let's do evil so that good may come. Beloved, good can never come out of evil doing.

NUGGET 20 - Fight The Good Fight Of Faith

Bible Reading: 1st Timothy 6:12
Fight the good fight of faith, lay hold on eternal life, whereunto thou art also called, and hast professed a good profession before many witnesses.

1 Corinthians 9:26, 1 Timothy 1:18, 2 Timothy 4:7, 2 Timothy 2:4.

In the scripture above, Apostle Paul enjoined us to fight a good fight of faith. A fight involves actions. Apostle Paul knew that Christian faith is all about actions and a fight between evil and good, powers of darkness and the children of light, righteousness and sin and a fight between the flesh and the spirit. There is a constant war between the flesh and the spirit and we must not let flesh nor sin win this battle.

Beloved this fight requires standing firm in the Lord, being rooted in Him and His words, obeying not your own body(flesh) nor depending on your human reasoning but solely on God's word, keeping God's commandments without spots, pursuing righteousness, godliness, having love, faith, patience and being gentle and blameless until the very end.

Also guard your heart and your mind which is the battle ground, the arena of the fight. It is in the mind that sin is formed for it is what you conceive in your heart that you put into actions, so guard the mind jealously for out of it flows the issues of life.

Arm yourself with the same mind as Christ. Christ suffered His body in order to gain His glory. You must therefore suffer the flesh to be able to fight a good fight, do not succumb to flesh, do not what it says but what the word says and what the Holy Spirit says; die to flesh. Do not live according to the flesh nor fulfill the lust thereof. In 2nd Timothy 2:4

Apostle Paul told us that a good fighter does not entangle himself with the affairs of the world so he might be able to please him that have chosen him. It is therefore important that as a good fighter we do not involve ourselves or get carried away by things of this world for worldliness is in enmity with God. God does not want us to be conformed to the world's pattern but to be different people in every way.

Apostle Paul fought and finished well. He fought a good fight and won. He was never distracted, he focused on eternal life even when trials, temptations and afflictions came, he looked unto God, the author and finisher of his faith. He held unto the promise of eternal life which was his ultimate goal.

Beloved, the person that will help us fight this fight is the Holy Spirit. Welcome Him, listen to Him, do His biddings and you will fight good and win big.

CHAPTER 3

Nugget 21
Hide The Word Of God

Nugget 22
The Lord Will Not Hear Me If...

Nugget 23
The Hairs Of Your Head Are Counted

Nugget 24
Christ Is Still Coming

Nugget 25
Abide In Him And He Will Abide In You

Nugget 26
Encounter God

Nugget 27
Let God Help You

Nugget 28
And They Cried And Their Cry Came Up To God

Nugget 29
What Manner Of Man Is This...

Nugget 30
All We Have Is Given To Us By God

NUGGET 21 - Hide The Word Of God In Your Heart To Avoid Sin

Bible Reading: **Psalms 119:11**
Thy word have I hid in my heart, that I might not sin against thee.

Joshua 1:8, Deuteronomy 6:6-9, Proverbs 1:7-16, Hebrews 4:12

Are you struggling with a particular sin, is there any particular habit in your life that God does not approve of that you are finding hard to get rid of. Beloved the word of God is what you need. The Psalmist said that he had hid the word of God in his heart so that he would not sin against God. God's word has the power to subdue sin in your heart. It is powerful, sharper than any two edged sword that pierces into the dividing asunder of marrows, joints, souls and spirits....(Hebrews 4:12). Those sinful thoughts that would not easily go away, the word of God in your heart can cut through them and bring them under subjection. Those long term formed bad and sinful habits that have defiled all manner of prayers, the word of God can extinct them and bring them to abrupt end.

The word of God in your heart is your power over sin. Just as the word of God has the power to heal, it also has the power to deliver and set free from sin for where the word of a King is, there is power; power against sin (Ecclesiastes 8:4). It is the word of God that you keep in your heart and remember that will actually keep you from sin when the opportunity to sin comes. The issue is, how much of the word do you know and how can you apply that word of God that you know to deliver and keep you from sinning against God.

Beloved, emulate the Psalmist who hid the word of God the best thing, in the best place which is his heart and for the best of purposes which is to avoid sinning against God. Whomever you love, you try not to off end. David loved God and did not want to displease Him so he hid His word in the most treasured part of him-the heart, to remember it, to reverence it and to practice it. God's word is the best preventive measure against off ending God, for it tells us His mind and His will, and it tends to bring our spirit into conformity with His.

Beloved, there is no better place to keep the word of God than the heart for if you keep it in your mouth only, it can be taken away. If you record it in your book, the book might get missing but if thou lay it up in your heart, as Mary did with the words of the angel (Luke 2:19), no enemy shall ever be able to take it away from you and that guides you to live a holy life.

NUGGET 22 - The Lord Will Not Hear Me If...

Bible Reading: Psalms 66:18
If I regard iniquity in my heart the Lord will not hear me.

Mark 11:26
But if ye do not forgive, neither will your Father which is in heaven forgive your trespasses.

We are all sinners according to the scriptures that said we have all sinned and have fallen short of the glory of God and that if we say we have no sin, we deceive ourselves and the truth is not in us. God hates sin, He cannot condone sin in any form but He has a remedy for sin and that is to confess and forsake them according to the scripture in 1 John 1:9 which stated that if we confess our sins He is faithful and just to forgive us our sins and to cleanse us from all unrighteousness.

Beloved God can forgive us our sins and hear our prayers but He will never hear us if we regard iniquity in our hearts. This means that if we hold sin(s) in our hearts, love it, cherish it, enjoy it, willingly do it, excuse it, hide it, hide and do it, then the Lord will definitely shut His ears to our prayers. We cannot fellowship freely with Him, we would loose contact with the Holy Spirit and cannot commune with Him because He will depart from our spirits and leaves us empty and powerless.

Apart from harbouring sins in our hearts and loving it, beloved, if we do not forgive those who trespass against us, the Lord will not forgive us our own trespasses even if we confess them. He will not hear nor answer our prayers either. God is Omniscient. He alone searches our hearts and He knows whether we have forgiveness in our hearts towards others. Some forgive verbally not inwardly and such attitudes hinder us from receiving forgiveness from God and answers to our prayers.

Therefore beloved, study the scriptures very well, taking note that the Lord will not listen to our prayers let alone answer if we do not forgive others. He will not even accept our worship, praises or thanksgivings. Follow the scriptures and be guided.

NUGGET 23 - The Hairs Of Your Head Are Counted

Bible Reading: **Mathew 10:30**
But the very hairs of your head are all numbered.

Beloved, are you still wondering whether God truly loves you considering the situations you are facing right now? Are you still wondering whether God is still God in your life knowing that that particular thing you have been asking God for is yet to be manifested? Are you wondering when that your dream job is going to come seeing that it has taken rather too long? Are you fed up because the enemy is still waging war against you despite all your prayers? Are you afraid that that enemy might eventually kill or destroy you? The scripture is reassuring you that apart from the fact that God is fighting for you, He also knows every single hair of your hairs. So relax! God has got your back.

God cares so deeply about you. He knows everything about you and everything that happens to you. God sees our lives from every side. He knows our ends from the very beginnings. He even knows your every thought. God never forgets His own. He never looses count of all our suff erings and what we are going through and that is why I know that He will always save you.

St Luke's version of the text scripture added that we should therefore fear not for we are more valuable than the sparrows. This means that if God can take care of the birds, the grasses and all other of His creatures that are of less value, He can take care of you for you are more valuable than the birds and the grasses. God knows when to come in and He will come at the right time to save just in time.

NUGGET 24 - Christ Is Still Coming

Bible Reading: John 24:3
And if I go and prepare a place for you I will come again and receive you unto myself; that where I am, there ye may be also.

Revelation 3: 11; 22:7,12, Mathew 24:43 -50, Mark 13:35, Luke 12:37 -39

Beloved let us not forget the fact that Jesus our saviour promised that He is coming back again for us, the righteous. The devil happens to be more aware of that and has so blinded the world and filled everywhere with so much activities to the extent that some Christians can even go through a whole day, to a week without remembering that Jesus is coming and to some this go on for months. Beloved it is not supposed to be so. We should always be conscious of the fact that Christ is coming and that He can appear at anytime. This continuous consciousness keeps us alert and away from sin. It gives us hope that we are not labouring in vain. We are to live as if Jesus is coming the next minute. Let us not be filled with activities and be caught up in the hustle and bustle of the days and forget the second coming of Christ.

The above scripture tells us that there is a place Jesus had gone to prepare for every child of God and He would be coming again to take them there to dwell so let us not forget that all the hustle and bustle ends here and not so important as such that we should put all our minds to it and forget the real thing which is the place Jesus is coming to take us to.

Heaven is real and hell is real, it does not matter if the whole world has forgotten about heaven and hell. The hard truth is that some people are going to hell and some are going to make it to heaven and where ever you find yourself at the end of your stay on earth is determined by the kind of life you lived on earth. Living a holy life will guarantee you a home in heaven at the end of your stay on earth. It is written that without holiness and righteous living no eyes will see the Lord.

NUGGET 25 - Abide In Him And He Will Abide In You

Bible Reading: **John 15:4**
Abide in me, and I in you. As the branch cannot bear fruit of itself, except it abides in the vine; no more can ye, except you abide in me.

Jesus is the vine and we are the branches of the vine. As there is no branch without a vine, there is no 'us' without Jesus. As the branch cannot stand alone without attaching itself to the vine so can we not stand alone without Jesus. As the branch cannot survive without being hooked to the vine so can we not survive or live without being connected to Jesus. As the branch cannot bear fruits or reproduce without being in the vine and receiving nutrients necessary for growth and reproduction so can we not bear fruits without being in Christ.

Beloved if you constantly stay, hooked up and connected to Jesus who is the vine, you will always look nourished, healthy and loved. Jesus will always be present in your life to help you whenever the need arises. He will help you bear fruits of righteousness, holiness, love and peace because you abided in Him who is the vine. But if you allow yourself to be tricked by the devil, the enemy to detach from the vine and abide alone you will start bearing fruit of bitterness, envy, anger, strife and such fruits grieve the Holy Spirit. The moment you leave the vine, you loose your source of nutrients and start to wither away because you are no longer connected to Jesus the source of your nutrients.

Beloved, from our text scripture we can see that we can practically do nothing without Jesus and we are nothing without Him so with this knowledge let us constantly be in Christ by depending on Him alone realising that our help comes from Him alone and not man or any other source. Continuous fellowship with Jesus, constant study of the word of God and genuine love for God and our fellow men will make us abide in Christ and He in us.

NUGGET 26 - Encounter God

Bible Reading: **Proverb 8:35**
For whoso findeth me, findeth life and shall obtain favour of the Lord.

Beloved there are people you will meet in life and your life will change for the better and there are people you may meet and the reverse would be the case but when you encounter God, your life will definitely make a meaning. We all need God at every point in life. When you encounter God, your life will change for the better, when you encounter God, He will give you a new name. Saul's name was changed to Paul when he encountered God and Jacob's name was changed to Israel when he encountered God.

Colossians 3:2 says, set your affections on things above and not on things on earth and that can only be possible in this world of today when you encounter God. It is so easy to be distracted and tossed away by the dangerous winds blowing in our societies today if we have not had an encounter with God. God will always shield and protect His own especially those who have met with Him personally. Are you seeking for positive popularity, when you encounter God, He will introduce Himself to you but He will use you, He will announce you to the world and launch you into greatness.

When you encounter God, He will always oversee your affairs, your battles will no longer be yours but His and He will fight for you when and where necessary.

Beloved, if you need to encounter God just make yourself available to Him. Live a life of obedience in even the littlest things He has commanded. Choose your friends wisely because God cannot come to you if you have bad friends. Seek God personally and develop a deeper relationship with Him and be faithful to anything He has committed into your hands.

NUGGET 27 - Let God Help You

Bible Reading: **Psalms 121:2**
My help cometh from the Lord which made heaven and earth.

**Genesis 49:25, Exodus 18:4,
Psalms 10:8; 20:2; 38:22; 46:1; 6: 11, Mathew 15:25**

Beloved, let the Lord help you. If you really desire and need good and perfect help from any kind of situation, be it help from powers that are stronger than you, be it help to come out of any form of addiction, be it help in your businesses, be it help in your homes, careers, jobs and children's lives; our help can only come from the one who made the heavens and the earth, the one who is stronger and mightier than us and the strongest powers.

Whenever the weak or the needy requires help, a stronger person is needed to off er that help, someone who has what it takes to help; one who has all the necessary equipment to help. Beloved, God has all it takes to help you.

Most of the problems we encounter in life are from the forces and powers of darkness in the heavens, earth, atmospheric air and the seas and that is why we need help from the one who created all these powers and forces and their dwelling places. He alone knows these powers that trouble us and He alone holds the keys to dealing with them. According to the scriptures, our help comes from the one who made the heavens and the earth. This means that if God created the heavens, He knows everything in the heavens and if He is the one who made the earth, He also knows everything on it including the powers that are in the heavens and those on the earth responsible for all the troubles we go through in life.

So beloved, key in to that God who has all it takes to help you and call upon Him and He will answer you and show you great and mighty things.

NUGGET 28 - And They Cried And Their Cry Came Up To God

Bible Reading: Exodus 2:23 -24
And it came to pass in process of time, that the king of Egypt died: and the children of Israel sighed by the reason of the bondage, and they cried and their cry came up to God by the reason of their bondage.
And God heard their groaning, and God remembered His covenant with Abraham, with Isaac and with Jacob.

Beloved, how do you feel when you hear the cry of your child? The way you feel when you hear your child cry is exactly the way God feels whenever He sees or hears you cry and when He sees you in pain and in need. The scriptures said that the children of Israel were in great bondage by a wicked Egyptian King and they cried to God and their cry came up to Him. The question now is what do we do when we are in pain? What do we do when we are in bondage, who do we consult and who do we go to. Do we cry to God or other gods, do we tell God who will hear our cry or friends who will laugh at us and carry our stories all around. Beloved the best thing to do is what the Israelites did; they cried unto God and He heard them and please note what God did. In verse 24 of Exodus 2, the scripture said that He remembered His covenant. This means that crying to God will make Him remember all His covenants He made to His children.

Beloved what is it that is making you cry, make sure you do not cry to any other but God because other gods and fellow human beings might not hear you or help you. God's shoulder is always available for you. Cry on His shoulder through prayers and supplications and He will hear your groaning and He will send your Moses to deliver you just like He did for the children of Israel.

Beloved who is it that is pursuing you, the scripture said in Psalms 56:9 that when you cry to God, that enemy that is pursuing you will turn back. So go ahead and cry to God and you will see what God can do.

NUGGET 29 - What Manner Of Man Is This...

Bible Reading: Mark 4:41
And they feared exceedingly, and said one to another, What manner of man is this, that even the wind and the sea obey him?

Beloved, we need to know Jesus, the power in Him and what manner of man He is to the extent that we do not bother about things or situations no matter how they look or present themselves. We need to know whom we believe in and who is with us in this our journey called 'life. Once we know that the one with us is Jesus, we do not fear what man or situations can do.

Jesus was with His disciples on a journey with a ship. There arose a great storm and Jesus was sleeping soundly and I believe He must have had a feeling that there was trouble but He was aware of the authority He has over the wind and the storms so He did not bother. He was also aware that the ship can never sink since He was there so He continued with His sleep. He wondered why His disciples could still be afraid of the storm, afraid that the ship would sink despite the fact that He was there with them.

In verse 40 of Mark 4, Jesus asked them "why are ye so fearful? How is it that you have no faith? This means that if they had removed fear. It also means that if they had realized that if He had done so many miracles before their very eyes that He can also calm the storm for them and they would not have been full of fear and disturbed His sleep. They would have handled the situation by a simple act of faith that they can never sink if Jesus is in their ship.

Beloved we need to know the manner of man, the captain of our ship, Jesus is and also the power He has and the power we have as the ones who have been authorized to use His powerful name.

NUGGET 30 - All We Have Is Given To Us By God

Bible Reading: **James 1:17**
Every good gift and every perfect gift is from above, and cometh down from the Father of lights, with whom is no variableness, neither shadow of turning.

John 3:27, Acts 3:6, Hebrews 5:4

Beloved every good thing we have or ever will have is given to us by God. He gives freely to all mankind regardless of background, ethnicity, faith or nationality and He gives not based on the works we have done or by our righteousness. Titus 3:5 says not by works of righteousness which we have done but according to His mercy He saved us. Romans 5:8 also said that He gave Christ for us all even while we were yet sinners.

Beloved let us be humbled by this great God and His ways and allow Him to move freely in our lives the ways He chooses to. Let us learn from Him and give freely to all men regardless of who they are.

CHAPTER 4

Nugget 31
Remain Faithful In Your Stewardship

Nugget 32
Sow Bountifully, Reap Bountifully

Nugget 33
The Devil Is An Accuser

Nugget 34
Be Focused

Nugget 35
Give No Room For Anxiety

Nugget 36
War

Nugget 37
Do Not Let Go

Nugget 38
Encourage Yourself In The Lord

Nugget 39
If You Love Me, Keep My Commandments

Nugget 40
Remember The Lord Thy God

NUGGET 31 - Remain Faithful In Your Stewardship

Bible Reading: **1st Corinthians 4:2**
Moreover it is required in stewards, that a man be found faithful.

Mathew 24:45; 25:23, Luke 12:42; 16: 11-12; 19:17, Galatians 5:22, P roverb 28:20

To be faithful means to be loyal, trustworthy, steadfast and to be committed. According to the scriptures, stewards are required to be faithful to their masters. God is our master and we are His stewards and we are required to be faithful in our ministries and to care for that which God our master has entrusted to us. We are required to preach and teach the gospel that had been delivered to us by God our master. We are to make it our responsibilities to share the good news of our Lord Jesus Christ to all.

Apart from preaching and teaching the gospel, we can also demonstrate faithfulness in our stewardships in the area of church planting and contributing to the growth of our local churches even to the cleaning of our church and its environs. God rewards such faithfulness. Let us therefore be faithful and remain faithful, it is worthwhile.

Carefully study the scriptures below and receive the grace to be faithful.

Mathew 25:21 the word of God says, "His lord said unto him, Well done, thou good and faithful servant; thou hast been faithful over a few things, I will make thee ruler over many things: enter thou into the joy of thy Lord."

2nd Chronicles 16:9 says "For the eyes of the Lord run to and fro throughout the whole earth, to shew Himself strong in the behalf of those whose heart is perfect towards Him...."

Proverb 28:20 says "A faithful man shall abound with blessings...."

NUGGET 32 - Sow Bountifully, Reap Bountifully

Bible Reading: **2 Corinthians 9:6**
But this I say, He which soweth sparingly shall reap also sparingly; and He which soweth bountifully, shall reap also bountifully.

Genesis 8:22, Psalm 126:5 -6, Galatians 6:7

There is a law that we reap in proportion to what we sow and in 2 Corinthians 9:6, Apostle Paul is not referring to reaping of material things in giving or sowing but the reaping has to do more of spiritual blessings of eternal glory.

Bountiful sowing leads to bountiful reaping and this operates both negatively and positively. When we sow abundantly to the spirit, we will reap abundantly spiritual blessings and when we sow sparingly, we would reap also according to the measures we have sown in spiritual blessings. The same applies to when we sow to the flesh and in actions; we reap in accordance with the fleshy sowing and reap the consequences of our actions.

David sowed in the flesh by admiring and lusting after his subject's wife and he reaped adultery in return. When he sent Uriah to the war front to be killed and he subsequently took his wife, he sinned greatly and he reaped great consequences for his action. Samson sowed to the flesh by mixing himself with an unbeliever and going as far as marrying her and he reaped greatly the consequences thereof.

The sowing also has to do with our times. Since the Lord Jesus Christ has given us years to spend on earth by His grace, we are to sow bountiful years of service in His kingdom using the talents and gifts He had given us to the edification of His body and to bringing souls to His kingdom. Beloved, we are to be a people who do not only sow bountifully of our possessions but our potentials, our talents, our lives, our times and our knowledge of the gospel and when we do, we reap abundant spiritually blessings from God.

NUGGET 33 - The Devil Is An Accuser

Bible Reading: **Zechariah 3:1**
And he showed me Joshua the high priest standing before the angel of the Lord and Satan standing at his right hand to resist him.

Revelation 12:10

The devil is envious that you are God's; he is envious that you are born again, he is envious that the blood of Jesus is still available for you; he is envious that you still have time to repent of your sins; he is envious and angry that your name has been written in the book of life. That is why he is always present to accuse you before the Lord just as the scripture explained.

Beloved, since we know that the enemy, the devil is envious of our relationship with God and therefore does not have good plans for us as children of God, what manner of Christians are we supposed to be. The scripture said that we are not ignorant of his devises and the tools he constantly uses to attack us. It is a known and established fact that the devil does not like us and wants our names to be erased from the book of life just like his was erased. Bearing the this fact in mind, we are not supposed to joke with our Christian lives, our relationships with Christ or lower our standards when it comes to sin. Sin and compromise are some of the tools the devil uses to mar our relationships with God just to make sure our names are removed from the book of life.

Beloved, God always have good plans for us but the devil is always there to resist those plans. We are to be alert and be vigilant to know when the devil is trying to creep into our lives to soil our relationship with God. When we loose our relationship with God, we loose God's plans for us and we scare away the angels He has sent to protect us and deliver our blessings to us. Let us be careful not to let the devil come between us and God.

NUGGET 34 - Be Focused

Bible Reading: **Hebrews 12:2**
Looking unto a Jesus, the author and finisher of our faith; who for the joy that was set before Him endured the cross, despising the shame, and is set down at the right hand of the throne of God.

Proverbs 22:29, Mathew 6:22 -24, 1 Corinthians 9:24 -27

Beloved, be focused; I know you must have mapped out plans, goals and objectives for the year and you know the devil so well that he too is aware of your plans and would set all his tools in motion to stop you from achieving your goals but whatever happens, do not loose focus.

The devils plans would be to kill, steal and destroy those plans you have made but be focused, looking unto Jesus, the author and finisher who has helped you form those plans and who will also help you finish and achieve your plans. Jesus had goals to bring salvation to mankind and to go back to His father with joy to sit at the right hand of His throne and because he had plans and goals He wanted to achieve, He endured trials, temptations and all

all that the devil, the destroyer of plans brought to Him. Jesus was focused. He was never deterred by what the devil would do or have done, He was never afraid of the devil and never gave in to his tricks and demands and at the end He became victorious.

Beloved, let us be like Jesus, who for the joy that was set before Him endured and was focused till the end.

NUGGET 35 - Give No Room For Anxiety

Bible Reading: **Philippians 4:6 -7**
Be careful for nothing but in every thing by prayer and supplication with thanksgiving let your requests be made known unto God. And the peace of God which passeth all understanding, will guard your hearts and minds through Christ Jesus.

Beloved, it is very natural to worry about certain things especially when things are not going as planned but our heavenly Father knows our worries and He cares about us and because He cares for us, He is always there to listen to what we will say to Him through prayers.

The scriptures have given us some advice on how to handle issues that come our ways so as to have peace in our hearts instead of worry and anxiety. The scripture first of all advised that we should not be anxious, we should put aside worry and anxiety and then pray, bringing up the issues before our heavenly Father and not forgetting to thank Him for the things He has earlier done.

After putting away worries and after praying, God will send His peace to your hearts to keep you. He will answer your prayers and sort all your issues out because you trusted He will do it by not worrying. So be not anxious about those issues in your live, relax and pray and God will send answers.

NUGGET 36 - War

Bible Reading: **Rev 12:7-8**
And there was war in heaven: Michael and his angels fought against the dragon; and the dragon fought and his angels.
And prevail not; neither was their place found any more in heaven.

TheThe above passage tells us that there was war in heaven meaning that there can be war even in a place as peaceful and as beautiful as heaven; a place where God Himself resides.

Beloved if the devil can tempt Jesus and if the devil and his cohorts can fight God it shows that they can also fight you, they can fight your home, they can fight your business, your ministry, your spiritual life inclusive.

You must know that for you to fulfill your destiny or reach your goals in life, you must fight the devil. The angels in heaven had to fight to establish the throne of heaven. It is very true that we are born to win but we are also born to fight because before there could be a winner there must be a fight and for you to win, you must first of all fight. Thanks be to our Lord Jesus Christ who leads us in this fight but beloved, righteousness is one of the tools to use in fighting this war. You cannot win this war if you do not have the necessary tools of which righteousness is one of them. Righteousness exalts you above that devil who is fighting you and enables God to come into that fight and assist you to win.

NUGGET 37 - Do Not Let Go!!!

Bible Reading: **Isaiah 25:4**
For thou hast been a strength to the poor, a strength to the needy in his distress, a refuge from the storm, a shadow from the heat, when the blast from the terrible ones is as a storm against the wall.

Beloved it is important that we do not let go on the hold we have on our father. He is the source of our strength. He is our pillar, our rock and He is our all in all. If you do let go of the one who gives you life, how shall you live; if you let go of the one who gives you joy, how shall you be happy; if you let go on the one who gives you strength, how are will you be strong and if you let go of the one who gives victory, how will you be able to pull through this wicked world full of atrocities, injustice and unfairness and how will you become a winner.

The scriptures said He is the strength to the poor and to the needy in distress; He is a refuge from the storm and a shadow from the heat when the blast of the terrible and the wicked ones is as a storm against the wall.

Beloved, if God is all of the above and more to us then how can we leave Him; how are we ever going to survive without Him. Please this is not the time to turn back; this is not the time to leave Him but the time to hold Him by His words and hold Him firmly like never before. He will show Himself as a the mighty one who assist us in winning battles.

NUGGET 38 - Encourage Yourself In The Lord

Bible Reading: **1st Samuel 30:6**
And David was greatly distressed; for the people spake of stoning him, because the soul of all the people was grieved, every man for his sons and for his daughters, but David encouraged himself in the Lord His God.

David was initially depressed but he did not continue in his sorrows, he did not go about telling people his problems to attract sympathy or pity, he did not consult other gods nor seek assistance from them, he did not just sit down and do nothing about his situation. He encouraged himself in the Lord.

Beloved, what do you do in extreme situations, what do you do when you have tried all that you know and yet the situation still remains the same. What do you do when you have prayed all the prayers you know how to pray and yet there seems to be no improvement on that situation. Just like David, encourage yourself in the Lord for if David could do it you too can do it.

You can encourage yourself in the Lord by letting the word of God you know minister to your heart reassuring you that if God has said it, He will do. You can also encourage yourself by letting that word of God you know bring joy into your heart instead of worry. Remind God what His word has said concerning the situation and most importantly speak, confess and believe those words and you will see a change in that situation.

NUGGET 39 - If You Love Me, Keep My Commandments

Bible Reading: **John 14:15**
If ye love me, keep my commandments.

Jesus is saying to us today through the scriptures that if we say we love Him we must keep His commandments.

Beloved, there are two things that truly confirm that we are children of God. First we must love God and secondly we must keep His commandments. These two are inseparable for we cannot say we love God and cannot keep His commands for whosoever you love, you obey to please.

The love of God is defined by keeping His commandments. Therefore in reference to loving God, there is no other love than a love that is expressed by obedience to the word of God. The love of God motivates us into action and that action is obedience to His commands. And those commandments of God are not burdensome, if we consider it a burden to abide by God's commandments then the love of God is not made perfect in us.

It is therefore a pleasure to those who truly love God to do His will and abide by His detects. God's commandments are found in His word and if we are ignorant of the word of God we cannot be said to truly love God and cannot say we are His children. In order to love God we must first know His commandments, true love of God drives us to the word of God. Let us therefore continually read the word of God and keep it in our hearts and abide by it and by so doing; we demonstrate that we love God.

NUGGET 40 - Remember The Lord Thy God

Bible Reading: **Deuteronomy 8:18**
But thou shalt remember the Lord thy God: for it is He that giveth thee power to get wealth, that He may establish His covenant which He sware unto thy fathers, as it is this day.

Beloved, it is a command by the scriptures and indeed a good thing to always remember the Lord your God in all that you do or set out to do. Often times, people get successful and they forget who is behind their successes; they forget that if it had not been the Lord who was on their sides, they would not have made it. They forget how rough it was and how much they cried to God for help and the Lord helped them. Some even go as far as forgetting the vows they made to God when they were in that desperate situation. This scripture is coming to us today as a reminder that we should always remember that if not for God it would not have been possible. Without God that job, that house, that life, that place and that person you have become today would not have been possible. Therefore we need to constantly have this at back of our minds acknowledging Him and giving Him thanks.

To remember God also means acknowledging Him in all your ways and the scripture says He will direct your paths.

The power to be wealthy is all in His hands, a cattle on a thousand hills are His and the earth too and the fullness thereof. Beloved wealth is of the Lord and not from anywhere else. Wealth from anywhere else will only bring so much trouble, sorrow, everlasting bondage and eternal destruction. So in your quest for wealth be it financial wealth, wealth in health, wealth in knowledge, experience and power, remember the Lord Thy God for the power to make wealth lies with Him.

CHAPTER 5

Nugget 41
Safety Is Of The Lord

Nugget 42
Surround Yourself With Good Friends

Nugget 43
God Will Fight For You Only If..

Nugget 44
We Shall Give Account Bible

Nugget 45
Give And It Will Come Back To You

Nugget 46
Be Wise As Serpents And As Harmless As Doves

Nugget 47
Do Not Give The Devil What He Wants

Nugget 48
Return To God

Nugget 49
Drop Worry, Take Up Faith

Nugget 50
There Is Joy Over One Soul That Repents

NUGGET 41 - Safety Is Of The Lord

Bible Reading: Proverb 21:31
The horse is prepared against the day of battle: but safety is of the Lord.

A horse has a great strength and it is used in battles but even with its strength there is a limit to what the great horse with a great strength can do to provide safety in the day of battle ; even though men may make all necessary preparations, take all necessary precautions some even give themselves extra form of protections from other gods but except the Lord build a house in vain do the builders build and except the Lord keep watch over a city, over a business, over a life or a person, in vain do the guards guard and in vain do the extra protections protect.

Beloved, we need God when it comes to safety. Only and only God protects, only Him gives victory in battles with the enemy and only Him provides safety. In any safety talks, there are conditions and guidelines to safety. In this context, trust and faith in the Lord are the conditions and guidelines that will guarantee us God's safety and preservation.

Our loving father preserves those who solely put their trust in Him. He knows they have no other but Him. He sees the needs of those who trust and obey Him. He delivers them from death and preserves them. He is their help in times of need and shield in times of assault by the wicked. The scriptures confirmed that those who trust in the Lord are like mount Zion which cannot be removed but abide forever. As the mountains are round about Jerusalem so the Lord is round about His people from henceforth even forevermore.

NUGGET 42 - Surround Yourself With Good Friends

Bible Reading: **1st Corinthians 15:33**
Be not deceived: evil communications corrupts good manners.

**Proverbs 27:17, Ecclesiastes 4:9 -12,
Proverbs 12:26; 17:17; 18:24; 22:24; 27:6,9**

Evil communication corrupts good manners, show me your friends and I will show you who you are. Whosoever you follow, you act like. Your constant companion depicts who you are and influences you to a large extent. Surround yourself with negative, valueless and evil minded people and you become and behave just like them. But follow good, valuable and positive minded people and you become and behave exactly like them; no wonder Christ followers were called Christians because they stayed with Him for so long and over time, they began to act, speak and behave like Him which made them to be called Christians meaning Christ-like.

Christ disciples had their different lives, behaviours and lifestyles before they met Jesus but when Jesus called them and they followed Him, they left their former lifestyles and behaviours and adopted Jesus' ways of life and characters. Beloved this simply shows that once you start following a person or get acquainted with a person you will be forced to drop your former nature and adopt the nature and lifestyle of whom you are following or whom you are acquainted with.

Therefore we have to be very careful who we choose as friends, acquaintances or mentors for it goes a long way in forming whom we are or whom we will become. For those of us who are parents, it is very important we monitor our children closely to know who they call friends because their characters and lifestyles now and in the future will be determined by who they follow or the type of friends they keep.

Beloved, apart from choosing our friends, let our best friend still remain Jesus. He is the sweetest and the best friend ever. With Jesus as our friend, we will never go wrong and our characters will be just like His.

NUGGET 43 - God Will Fight For You Only If..

Bible Reading: Exodus 14:14
The Lord shall fight for you and ye shall hold thy peace.

God is always there to fight for His children and defend them whenever the need arises but He can only fight for us if we allow Him to and not fight for ourselves. Several times we call God into our battles to fight for us but we do not let Him do it His own ways; we still interfere by trying to fight the battle ourselves.

Beloved, for God to absolutely fight our battles we need to solely hand over to Him and hands off. You have prayed, you have fasted and you applied faith and you have stopped worrying then patiently wait and watch while He fights for you; do not engage in anything that will cause Him to cease the fight on your behalf.

Also God can only fight for you if your hands are clean for the scripture says that only the man with a clean hands shall ascend into the hill of the Lord. You cannot ask God to fight for you when your hands are soiled with blood or when you are the guilty party in the fight for God is a righteous judge. He will not fight that battle but will leave you to it. So beloved hand over the battle to God and leave Him to fight for you. Do not fight the battles you have asked God to fight.

NUGGET 44 - We Shall Give Account

Bible Reading: **Romans 14:12**
So then every one of us shall give account of himself to God.

Mathew 12:36; 18:23; 25:19, Luke 16:12,
Hebrews 4:13; 13:17, 1 Peter 4:5

Beloved, we are not in this world to just come and go. There is nothing like man come, man die, man go. There is an eternal destination for every one after life. At the end of life, everyone is expected to appear before God, the owner and giver of lives to give account of how the life He gave us to live was spent here on earth and this will happen immediately after life. The scripture said it is appointed unto man once to die and after that comes judgement.

Every random thought, every idle words, every righteous and unrighteous impulse, every secret and open prayer, every hidden and unhidden deeds, long-forgotten sin, act of compassion and act of good will be brought into the open for us to acknowledge. Open for the Lord to judge and for the appropriate recompense to be given which is heaven for the good and hell fire for the bad. I pray we will never be judged into hell.

However beloved, remember that even after making heaven, after the judgement, we shall also be judged on our services and works unto the Lord. This judgement is an assessment of worth and it is with a reward. This judgment is an evaluation of faithfulness and service within God's family. This judgement is based on motives behind our labour in God's vineyard and the reason for working for God. If we are working to be seen and praised by men and if we are working for God to build His kingdom, all of that will be judged.

Our works would also be judged based on the level of faithfulness of how faithful we are in our services unto the Lord. So let us therefore be mindful of how we live our lives and how we work for God because one day, we will give account of it all.

NUGGET 45 - Give And It Will Come Back To You

Bible Reading: **Luke 6:38**
Give, and it shall be given unto you; good measure, pressed down, and shaken together, and running over, shall men give into your bosom. For the same measure that ye mete withal it shall be measured to you again.

Matthew 5:42; 10:42, Psalm 37:21, P roverbs 22:9; 28:27, Ecclesiastes 11:1-6

Beloved, in terms of giving our money and material things either for the propagation of the gospel of our Lord Jesus Christ or for our fellow men it is only logical for us to tighten up our giving but we should not relent in giving for God will still provide our needs.

Apart from giving our money and material things we should also note that giving is not all about that, it goes beyond that. The scripture says give and it shall be given back to you. This means that when you give you shall definitely receive back and in that case we should be careful of what we give for it will surely come back to us.

Just as we receive back when we give money or material things, we shall also receive back when we give love, kindness, affection even good and bad deeds. Also note that the receiving is also accompanied with the measure or quantity with which we give. So we should also be aware of the quality and quantity of our giving for we shall also receive same back.

Let us therefore give in positive ways for whatever we give shall surely come back to us with the same quantity and quality with which we have given.

NUGGET 46 - Be Wise As Serpents And Harmless As Doves

Bible Reading: **Mathew 16:10**
Behold, I send you forth as sheep amongst wolves:
be ye therefore wise as serpents, and harmless as doves.

Psalm 19:7; 101:2, P roverbs 4:7; 13:14; 20:18; 21:20, Proverbs 22; 24:5,6, Ecclesiastes 7:12

Wisdom is the principal thing. One wise man is better than hundreds of fools put together. A decision of a wise man is always right, full of wisdom and good reasoning. A wise man is discreet in all his ways and a good forecaster. A wise man sees the devil first before he sees him. A wise man goes a step ahead of the devil and the devil cannot outwit him or lure him into sin. He cannot fall into the devil's trap because he sees the devil and his evil plans ahead of time no matter how and runs away before he catches him.

Jesus is admonishing us today to be very wise as He sends us into the evil world. He knows what kind of world we are in; a world full of all kinds of wickedness but one of the principal tools we need to survive the wolves in the world is wisdom. The scripture says "get it". As children of God called by Him unto good works we need to be wise, we need wisdom from above so as to know when, what and how when it comes to dealing with the devil and the wolves.

Beloved we need wisdom in our daily walks and works with the Lord on this earth because there are so many sugar coated off ers out there especially in this end time and if we are not wise enough to know that this is actually from the devil and the pit of hell we will fall prey and loose Jesus, our blessings and our heavenly home and our rewards. God forbid!

Jesus also said we should be as harmless as doves. This means we should be symbols of peace and innocence, we should be clean hearted and of clean hands, and we should be harmless, do no one any harm. We should be without blemish so that at the end, He would present us to His father as living sacrifices holy and acceptable unto Him.

NUGGET 47 - Don't Give The Devil What He Wants

Bible Reading: Ephesians 4:27
Neither give place to the devil.

Do not give room to the devil, do not oblige him his desires, he is forever of no good and never means well for any of God's children. He hates God's children with great passion and is always scheming to bring them down. The mission of the devil on earth is to kill, steal and to destroy. Beloved, do not allow him.

If the devil wants to kill you do not allow him. Tell him the word of God that your life is hid in Christ and in God. If he wants to steal your joy, your blessings and all that God has rightfully given you, do not let him. Tell him that God has blessed you with every spiritual blessings in heavenly places and that all you have is given to you by God and not him. If he wants to destroy your body with sicknesses, tell him that your body is the living temple of Christ and that you are healed by the stripes of Jesus. If he wants you and your soul, tell him that you are Christ's and that you are sitting with Christ in heavenly places far above him and sins.

Beloved, anything at all the devil wants from you, do not give him. Do not give him the opportunity to laugh at you or accuse you before God and most importantly do not let him meet you in hell, a place meant only for him and his angels.

NUGGET 48 - Return To The Almighty

Bible Reading: Job 22:23&24
If thou return to the Almighty, thou shalt be built up, thou shall put away iniquity far from thou tabernacles. Then thou shalt lay up gold as dust and the gold of Ophir as the stones of the brooks.

Beloved have you in any way abandoned your creator, the Almighty. Have you allowed the cares of this world to delete your faith in God? Have you said in your heart that the Lord has delayed so much in bringing His promises to pass in your life? Have you waited for God to answer that particular prayer and it seems He is not and you have decided to go your own way? Have you thought in your heart that God does not answer prayers. Are you planning to go back to Egypt because you have seen the wicked prospering more than the righteous? Beloved, understand that the devil has set up all these strategies to lure you away from God and to himself.

Please do not go away from the Almighty. The scriptures is telling u you today to return unto Him and you shall be built up. Put away iniquity far away from you and God will bless you with gold and with silver. God cannot lie, it might take long but He must surely fulfill His promises, all it takes is perseverance.

There are so many other benefits you can gain by holding unto God. Job 22:25 said that the Lord shall be your defense which means that He will protect you from all harms and defend you from your enemies and not only you but all that concerns you. The scriptures further said that He shall answer your prayers, He shall cause everything you decree to be established and He shall cause His light to shine upon your ways. Even when men are saying there is a casting down, hunger and troubles in the land, you shall be singing a different song of praise unto Him.

NUGGET 49 - Drop Worry, Take Up Faith

Bible Reading: **1st Peter 5:7**
Casting all your care upon Him; for He careth for you.

Beloved, worry is a sin, worry causes unbelief; it is a burden to the heart. Worry takes one to nowhere but to the world of tiredness, sickness and disease; it is like a rocking chair that will make you loose energy and get you tired but with no distance covered. Worry will do you no good and it is interesting to note that most things we sit down and take time to worry about does not even get solved until we drop worry and take up faith. Worry is like telling God "God do you know what? Keep off let me handle it". Worry is taking God out of the situation and failing to remember the promises of God and His faithfulness.

Philip in John 6:7, did not not recognise that he was with Jesus, the bread of life himself when he was worried about the amount of money that would be sufficient to feed the multitude that followed Jesus. Andrew also in verse 9 of John chapter 6 did not recognise the miraculous nature of Jesus when he was worried that the food they had at that present would not be enough to feed so many. Beloved if you are with Jesus, you need not to worry. Just drop that worry at the feet of Jesus and He will give you rest in place of that worry for the scripture says: come unto me all of you that are heaven laden and I will give you rest.

NUGGET 50 - There Is Joy Over One Soul That Repents

Bible Reading: **Luke 15:10**
Likewise I say unto you, there is joy, in the presence of the angels of God over one sinner that repenteth.

Beloved do you know that the only time the hosts of heavens rejoice is when just one sinner repents; this shows that God loves sinners to be saved and how can they be saved. Most of them probably have never heard about Christ, some of them are in our offices, Workplaces, neighbourhood and all around us and what are we doing to cause heavens to rejoice over them.

This also means that the heavens knows how terrible hell is and will immediately celebrate each time a soul escapes hell.

If for your actions and words someone goes back to sin and ends up in hell fire, think of how sad heavens will be and how God will feel towards you and of course how will you be able to explain that to God on the last day. So why not cause joy in heaven today and cause a sinner to repent through your preaching, evangelism or through your lifestyles.

Apart from causing the heavens to be in rejoicing and celebrations mode, you will also have rewards for yourselves and one of the rewards amongst others is that since whatever a man's sows he reaps, you will reap joy and celebrations here on earth. Heavens will cause joy never to cease in your hearts; each time you see your converts your hearts rejoice and that joy spreads to all other areas of your lives. Also because God is happy with you, He answers your prayers expressly. So win souls today and enjoy your rewards!

CHAPTER 6

Nugget 51
And He Withdrew Himself

Nugget 52
Greater Love

Nugget 53
You Need Power

Nugget 54
Beauty For Ashes; Sadness For Joy

Nugget 55
Be Still!

Nugget 56
Prayer Works

Nugget 57
The Power Of Intercession

Nugget 58
God Is A Master Planner

Nugget 59
What Words Do You Speak

Nugget 60
We Are Blessed!

NUGGET 51 - And He Withdrew Himself

Bible Reading: **Luke 5:16**
And He withdrew himself into the wilderness, and prayed.

Beloved, it is important to create a quiet time for God, it will be better and beneficial to us if we build a place for God too not only in our hearts but in our abodes. When you have a place of prayer, it will be difficult for you to go by the day without kneeling to God to commune with Him. Creating a quiet time might be difficult in this time due to tight schedules and the need to make ends meet but Jesus our role model even though He is the son of God and was quite busy with the work of His father still had a quiet time for God.

According to the word of God, Jesus withdrew himself into the wilderness and prayed. This scripture is worth learning from. Jesus understood the great importance of creating a quiet and special time for God that He had to leave everything and away from distractions to commune with His father. He did not consider the fact that since He and His father are one that He will hear Him anyways whether He prayed or not. Jesus had everything. He had powers, He had authority and needed absolutely nothing because He had it all but He still withdrew Himself and prayed.

The need to create time for God cannot be overemphasized even if we have everything, even if we are very busy and even if we have attained advanced stages in our spiritual and Christian lives. God needs our time. He cannot force us into a relationship with Him but He is constantly itching to hear from us and if we create time for Him, He will create time for us, if we draw near to Him, He will draw near to us.

We can only find God in stillness and quietness. We can only hear God when we are still and quite with full focus and concentration on Him voiding ourselves of distractions. Seek God today in such manner and you will find Him.

NUGGET 52 - Greater Love

Bible Reading: **John 15:13**
Greater love hath no man than this, that a man lay down his life for his friends.

Jesus love is what is described as the 'agape' type of love. It is the highest form of love. According to John 15:13, Jesus love is so great that He laid down His life for those referred as His friends.

Beloved, when the scripture talked about Jesus loving His friends in a manner that led Him to lay down His life for them, it was referring to you and I. It is a great honour to be called Jesus' friends and even a greater honour for Him to lay down His life for us. If Jesus was able to lay down His life for us which is the greatest sacrifice ever, how can He then not freely and easily give us all things we desire from Him.

Jesus is a role model to us and we should follow this example of love that He has shown us. His love should teach us to love in like manner, those we call our friends even our enemies. Jesus went an extra mile to demonstrate His love, we too should not hesitate to demonstrate our love for one another whenever the need arises.

We did not do anything for Him to deserve that kind of love yet He loved us in that manner. Likewise, we should love others without expecting to be loved in return and without reservations.

Jesus loves every race and gender regardless and that should teach us not to discriminate against others and not to treat people different. Everybody received equal agape love from Jesus. The love that has been made available to everyone who believes, to everyone who received and to every woman and man upon the earth.

That agape kind of love teaches us to forgive one another even when there is no reason to and even when the forgiveness is not deserved. Jesus gave His life for us even while we were yet sinners.

Beloved, let us enjoy that agape love from Christ and at the same time exhibit such love one for another.

NUGGET 53 - You Need Power

Bible Reading: **Acts 1:8**
But ye shall receive power and after that the Holy Ghost is come upon you: and ye shall be witnesses unto me both in Jerusalem, and in all Judea, and in Samaria, and unto the uttermost part of the earth.

Beloved we need the power of God in this end times and receiving that ultimate power from God is very paramount in our christian journey. No matter how powerful and beautiful and sophisticated a car is without a petrol that car will be very difficult to move so also no matter how close we claim to be with God and no matter how many years we claim to have known Christ without that ultimate power at work in us we will not make significant progress in our walks with God. We cannot make an impact in this world for the kingdom.

This same principle also applies when it comes to accomplishment of purpose. Every soul is given a goal to accomplish here on earth but if we do not have what it takes to accomplish that purpose we may waste our stay on earth.

There are so many powers in this world but the most important to those who are born of water and spirit is the ultimate power which will enable them to reign, dominate and subdue the earth.

When Jesus was on earth his disciples did enjoy privileges of cover and protection and power but when He was leaving the earth, He told them that they need power to carry on as He was leaving them. He told them to go nowhere until they have received that power. The power that will drive them to move from Jerusalem to all other parts of the world, to dominate and to preach the word.

Beloved we need the power of the Holy Ghost which is the ultimate power. If there is no power, there is no success and there is no movement. We need power to preach the gospel of our Lord Jesus to all men and to get our needs easily met. According to the scriptures, the easiest way to get something quickly and easily from God is through evangelism. We also need that power to make wealth, to protect ourselves and our families. We need that power for the fulfillment of our destiny and to assist us live holy and conquering Christian lives.

Beloved desire for that power; ask God for that power, sincerely hunger for it, study the word of God and sanctify yourself by living right and the Lord will give you that power.

NUGGET 54 - Beauty For Ashes; Sadness For Joy

Bible Reading: Isaiah 61:3
To appoint unto them that mourn in Zion, to give unto them beauty for ashes, the oil of joy for mourning, the garment of praise for the spirit of heaviness; that they might be called trees of righteousness, the planting of the Lord, that He might be glorified.

Psalms 30: 11
Thou hast turned for me my mourning into dancing, thou hast put off my sackcloths and girded me with gladness.

Beloved God is an expert when it comes to trade by barter; He is a grand exchanger. The scripture above tells us that He can trade our beauty for ashes, He can trade our joy for mourning, and He can trade our garment of praise for the spirit of heaviness.

God's story is about making the bad things untrue and turning them into good. He makes beauty out of brokenness. God's biggest gift to His people is transforming their pains to joy. He does not desire and cannot bear to see any of His children suffering.

Beloved, let this knowledge of God's plan and desires for you allow you to live your life joyfully, despite the brokenness all around you. No matter what sadness we face today, we can remain joyful because we have the hope and knowledge that whatever sadness we face today, our God can exchange sadness for joy!

The Psalmist had that knowledge that was why he turned a prayer of deliverance to praise in Psalms 30:11; he looked into the future where he would praise God forever. So beloved see praise in that problem, see joy in that pain because God can exchange that problem to praise and that pain to joy.

NUGGET 55 - Be Still!

Bible Reading: **Psalms 46:10**
Be Still and know that I am the lord, I will be exalted among the heathen, I will be exalted in the earth.

Beloved, have you ever seen a still water? It is usually calm. If you throw a stone inside a still water, a ripple would form but it still remains still. A still water is not moved by the wind either, it remains still.

To be still means to be calm, undisturbed, untroubled, unruffled or unmoved. It is important to remain still in times of trouble for it is only when you are still that the Lord will fight for you as it is written in Exodus 14:14. Most of us want God to fight our battles but we are not able to stand still and let Him fight instead we worry, we fret, we loose hope and loose faith.

It is only when you remain still in the midst of trouble that you will be able to hear that small still voice of God telling you what to do in that situation and how to handle it. It is only a calm mind that will reason well in times of trouble. It is only a calm mind that will make the right decisions in times of trouble. It is only a still mind that will be focused enough to know the right approach to conquer the enemy and gain victory from God. It is only a still mind that will be void of fear and capable enough to apply faith in order to get healed from sicknesses or get delivered from any kind of trouble. It is only a calm spirit that will receive from God. It is only a calm mind that will receive a word from God concerning any matter.

We know that it is only natural to feel troubled and agitated when problems come. Fear and doubt always try to overwhelm us when troubles come but always remember that God speaks in a small still voice and always a present help in times of trouble even if He delays there is always a reason for His delay. He is always there even when the storm is raging just looking at you to see your reactions and once it is time, He will come to your rescue.

Beloved it requires only to be still to see His salvation that was why He told the children of Israel to be still and they will see His salvation. Just remain calm, do not give in to fear and the Lord shall fight for you and victory shall be yours.

NUGGET 56 - Prayer Works

Bible Reading: **John 14:14**
If ye ask anything in my name, I will do it.

Beloved, in kneeling we win. There are so much wars and battles going on in the realm of the spirit by the kingdom of darkness against the children of God. Many have fallen out of faith due to lack of power to combat the devil, to face the devil squarely and to win the war. Many have become victims of the war, bartered, bruised and defeated. The reason for this is not farfetched- prayerlessness.

A prayerless child of God is often referred to as a powerless child of God. Beloved, prayer makes you powerful. The scriptures said that the weapons of our warfare are not canal but mighty through God for the pulling down of strongholds and these weapons cannot be activated without prayer. God is a very great God, the most powerful and the one who holds the whole universe. It is through prayer you can connect to that most powerful God and join Him to rule and control the universe.

The fire of the enemy do not burn a prayerful Christian just Shadrach, Meshach and Abednego rather it introduces the fourth man in the fire, Jesus for protection. A Prayerful Christian closes the mouth of the lion and the enemies. A prayerful Christian opens the doors of breakthrough and advertises the power of God just like in the case of Daniel. A Prayerful Christian breaks the chains of darkness just like Paul and Silas. A prayerful Christian communicates with God more, gets closer to God and builds a stronger relationship with God. If you are very close to God, He reveals secrets to you. He unveils His powers for you to do exploits and sanitizes your environment so no evil could devour you. He hides you under His shadows and gives His Angels charge over you and all your aff airs.

The scriptures said we should ask anything good and God would do it. How can we ask without prayer. How can we win battles if we do not ask God to intervene through prayers. It is through prayer we communicate with God and make our request known to Him.

Beloved, ask and you shall receive.

NUGGET 57 - The Power Of Intercession

Bible Reading: **Job 42:10**
And the Lord turned the captivity of Job, when he prayed for his friends: also the Lord gave Job twice as much as he had before.

Beloved, there is power in intercession. Intercession is a prayer offered to God on behalf of another person. It is that prayer you prayed to God about the sick, the oppressed, the leaders of your country, the church of God, your relatives, your friends saved and unsaved and even your enemies. The prayer of intercession paves ways for open doors, deliverance, blessings and all other benefits to the individual offering the prayers.

Often times, when we pray to God and we go on and on about our problems forgetting that that next door neighbour of ours needs prayer too. Some countries are in all kinds of troubles today because no one remembers to pray. Some of our family members are unsaved because we as Christians, do not care so much about their spiritual needs and do not pray for them. Many children are not living their destinies because some parents have got no time to pray for them.

The scripture explained that it was when Job prayed for his friends that the Lord turned his captivity, made him regain all that he lost and made him twice richer. This shows us that God always wants for us to pray for others and it might just be the only thing left for you to do for that long awaited miracle or blessings to manifest. It might be that God wants you to pray for that someone to be delivered so that your own deliverance will come or be complete.

So beloved, go ahead and pray for that someone who needs that prayer and watch God turn that captivity of yours just like He did for Job.

NUGGET 58 - God Is A Master Planner

Bible Reading: 1st Peter 5:10
But the God of all grace who hath called us unto His eternal glory by Christ Jesus, after that ye have suffered a while, make you perfect, establish strengthen, settle you.

Beloved, God is a trainer and a Master Coach. Just like an eagle trains his children to fly so does God train His children to be strong and rise above the devil and every circumstances. He is an expertise coach who uses means deemed fit for Him and suitable enough for His children to train them and when He is done training them, they come out revived, revitalised, perfected, strengthened, strong, established and settled.

God is a strategic planner. Immediately you give your life to Him and becomes His own, He starts to plan your life for you. Though most times His plans for us are totally out of our own plans but His plans are always better at the end. Most of us tactically deprive our children somethings that can harm them in the future though they love those things so much but because we want the best for them now and in the future, we do not let them have them. So does God deal with us His children. Most things we cry for God to give us He does not because He is all knowing God who knows the end from the very beginning and He wants us to have the best future.

Also there are things we know our children need and we can comfortably give them but because we want to teach them values that they do not just take things they want without asking for permission first so we do not give them without them asking first. We want them to ask before we can give them. In the same way, God wants us to ask for things He knows we definitely need just to train us on certain principles.

So beloved, let us not be in despair or distressed when our father is training us for He means well.

NUGGET 59 - What Words Do You Speak

Bible Reading: **Proverb 18:21**
Death and life are in the power of the tongue, and they that love it shall eat the fruit thereof.

Beloved the tongue is a powerful part in our body, out of it life can flow and out of it death can flow too. The tongue forms our words and words carry power. With words we can build and with words we can destroy. God used mere words to create the earth and everything in it. Words carry purpose. For every word God send to you is to accomplish something in our lives, to accomplish a purpose. God's word has a healing purpose, it has a deliverance purpose and it has a creating purpose. Beloved with the word of God you can create anything you desire, you can shape your life and destiny with the word of God.

Words are messengers and as messengers words can fulfil a mission of either life or death. The powers of darkness use words to accomplish their destructive purposes, they can send words as messengers to harm their victims. You too as a child of God can send words to destroy their destructions and prevent their harm coming to you.

Spoken words are very powerful, they can come to pass; they can make or mar. That is why you must reject immediately every evil word spoken against you and be careful of what you say.

It is important beloved, to cultivate the habit of speaking good words into your life every morning when you wake up to shape your day towards good accomplishments. Words also have entrance power, they can enter you and begin to manifest as spoken, that is why you must speak contrary words into your life once you notice that somethings are not right in your body or your endeavours because unknown to you the enemy might have spoken evil into your life.

Beloved be vigilant and wise to speak good words anytime, any day into your life and those words will come to accomplishment because words have accomplishing powers.

NUGGET 60 - We Are Blessed!

Bible Reading: **Ephesians 1:3**
Blessed be the God and father of our Lord Jesus Christ, who hath blessed us with all spiritual blessings in heavenly places in Christ.

Beloved, We are blessed already as the scriptures referred by using a past tense (blessed). Whosoever God has blessed. there is no curse whatsoever. To be blessed by God and father of our Lord Jesus Christ means you lack nothing, you are favoured, you are elevated, you have everything He thinks you need and you are contented. God is a spirit and His blessings are spiritual which are manifested physically to us. Those spiritual blessings include spiritual gifts He has endowed us with namely love, faith, peace, goodness, prophesy, healing and so on.

God blessing us with spiritual blessings in heavenly places means that, the sorts of blessings He has given us, are such that are found in heaven which includes good health, prosperity, peace, joy, righteousness to mention but a few. Beloved, these blessings have been made available for us to enjoy by our loving father. The only thing to do is to call down those blessings with faith; call the spiritual into the physical and they will manifest and be all yours to enjoy. Please take particular note of the part of the scripture that said He hath blessed us with all spiritual blessings in heavenly places in Christ. This simply means that you must continually be in Christ to be able to access fully these blessings. Please do not leave Him and the blessings will be yours.

CHAPTER 7

Nugget 61
God Ways Are Completely Different From Ours

Nugget 62
Praise To God Continually

Nugget 63
He That Walketh With The Wise Shall Be Wise

Nugget 64
The Benefits Of Fasting

Nugget 65
An Expected End

Nugget 66
Need For Revival

Nugget 67
God Of Jacob Is Our Refuge

Nugget 68
No Condemnation

Nugget 69
Mortify The Deeds Of The Body

Nugget 70
Be Persistent!

NUGGET 61 - God Ways Are Completely Different From Ours

Bible Reading: **Isaiah 55:8**
For my thoughts are not your thoughts; neither are your ways my ways saith the Lord.

Beloved, God's ways are higher than our ways and His thoughts higher than ours. God chooses the things that look foolish in our eyes to shame the wise. He also chooses those things we consider weak and powerless to shame the strong and the powerful. We serve a God who was not made by man. The Ancient Of Days, the one who formed the brain, created the most intelligent brains, the one who made the wisest and the greatest thinkers of our days. We cannot fathom the thoughts of God. The foolishness of God is wiser than men and the weakness of God is stronger than men.

The preaching of the gospel, the shedding of the blood, the death of God's only begotten son on the cross pointed out the fact that God is wiser. Also the fact that salvations comes by mere believing in the gospel that Jesus, God's only begotten son shed His blood and died on the cross tells us that God indeed is the wisest and chooses the foolish things to confound the wise. To the Greeks and the Jews, the whole salvation process sounds foolish but it is the true mystery of our faith and the wisdom of God.

Beloved let us view the above scripture from another angle. If God's thoughts are higher than our thoughts it then means that the good thoughts we are thinking for ourselves are nothing compared to the thoughts our good God is thinking concerning us. Also if your enemies are thinking evil thoughts concerning you, God's thoughts are way too much higher than their thoughts towards you and therefore shall not stand and shall not come to pass. Also when it comes to God's ways, they are different too. God's ways of visiting, answering and leading us are completely different from the way we expect.

Relax child of God and let God lead the way and let His thoughts prevail by committing your ways into His hands and asking Him to have His ways in your life.

NUGGET 62 - Praise To God Continually

Bible Reading: Hebrews 13:15
By Him therefore let us offer a sacrifice of praise to God continually, that is, the fruit of our lips, giving thanks to His name.

By Him therefore let us offer a sacrifice of praise to God continually, that is, the fruit of our lips, giving thanks to His name.

Beloved when we pray to God, most of the time we omit praising God or we praise Him just a little and suddenly start demanding this and that from Him. In most cases, we forget that we serve a powerful God who deserves to be recognized and admired, worshipped, praised and honoured for His love, power, and grace upon us.

The scriptures admonished us to offer sacrifices of praise continually to God and this means whether we have needs to ask of Him or not and it also means we should not cease, we should let the sacrifices of our praises flow to Him always. So beloved, as we go about our businesses each day, let us always fill our hearts and lips with praises unto Him, He deserves them.

Therefore beloved, do not forget when you go to Him in prayers, first spend some time and tell Him how much you love, adore and honour Him. Is God not glorious? Has He not done a lot? Count your blessings and name them one by one and it will surprise you how much He has done!

NUGGET 63 - He That Walketh With The Wise Shall Be Wise

Bible Reading: **Proverb 13:20**
He that walketh with the wise men shall be wise but a companion of fools shall be destroyed.

Beloved, you are your friends therefore choose your friends wisely; evil communication corrupts good manners. If you walk with the wise even though you were not born wise, over time the wisdom of your friends will influence and affect your life and you too will become wise. So also if you walk with fools and even though you are full of wisdom, your wisdom will fade away as you continue to associate with fools.

From the scriptures, we are able to deduct that fools end up in destruction. So many children of a God have been misdirected, some have fallen out of faith and some are heading to eternal doom because they mingled themselves with foolish friends and allowed themselves to be inclined negatively. Beloved show me your friends and I will show you who you are.

Let us be guided and allow the spirit of God tell us who is who and whom to choose as friends and whom not to choose as friends. We also have to be careful even when it comes to choosing business partners. The progress, products or profits of our businesses largely depend on whom we call business associates. Our destinies also is mostly determined by the company we keep.

Therefore examine your circle of friends now and evaluate how much impacts they have had in your life or how positively they have influenced you and consider whether it is time to change them or not.

NUGGET 64 - The Benefits Of Fasting

Bible Reading: **Joel 2:12**
Therefore also now, saith the Lord, turn ye even to me with all your heart, and with fasting, and with weeping, and with mourning:

Fasting involves abstinence from food. It is a means of bringing our flesh into submission to the Lord so He can strengthen us to overcome flesh and put all carnal temptations into subjection. Fasting subdues our flesh and elevates our souls. When we fast, our souls are constantly connected with God and this helps us to abstain from sin. When we fast, we become more aware of what is good and bad, we go to God without hindrance of any sort. No wonder we receive more revelations, receive more spiritual gifts and exercise our already given spiritual gifts more when we fast.

When we fast, the pain in our stomachs reminds us that Jesus is the true food, not our daily bread, that Jesus is the true drink, not our daily drinks. Fasting satisfies our souls' hunger and quenches our souls' thirst (John 6:35)

Beloved, Christian fasting is not mainly about what we go without, but who we want more of; fasting shows that we want more of God; He himself, in Christ, is the one who satisfies more than the best of foods, and quenches our thirst more than the purest of water, the richest of milk, and the best of wine. In him, our souls eat what is good and is satisfied and healthy, ready to commune with Him.

Fasting when added to prayers is required when asking God to deal with certain issues in our lives including long outstanding difficult situations (Mathew 17:21). God does not only reward us with what we ask of Him during fasting but He also rewards us of who He is as our desire, enjoyment, fulfillment and satisfaction.

Beloved, are you aware that; demonic and satanic agents fast too to upgrade their powers and levels; if they can do that, we Christians should engage more in fasting to upgrade ourselves spiritually.

NUGGET 65 - An Expected End

Bible Reading: **Jeremiah 29: 11**
For I know the thoughts that I think toward you, saith the Lord, thoughts of peace and not of evil, to give an expected end.

Beloved, everyone born on the surface of the earth has a path written for them by their maker; everyone has an expected end and that expected end is only known by God, the maker. Ignore the fortune tellers, the seers and those that claim they see the future. Your future is in His hands and He alone holds your future and that is why you must hold Him firmly because what you will become lies with Him.

Beloved, since your future is in God's hands, you have to follow the path that will release that future into your hands; you must let Him lead you to your future or how else can you achieve anything including your divine future except by Him. The scriptures recorded that man cannot receive anything except if it is given to him by God and that except the Lord builds a city in vain do the builders build.

However there are conditions to follow for you to have that expected end.

You must constantly dwell in the secret place of the most high, you must pray constantly to your maker to activate that future, you must be a friend of your maker and you must have confidence and faith in your maker that you will get there. You must not allow your present circumstances to overwhelm you or make you loose focus and mar your future. Also dream big, expect big, believe and see nothing less than beautiful future for yourself because if God has said He will give you an expected end, a hope and a future, surely He will for He cannot lie. Beloved, your future is bright.

NUGGET 66 - Need For Revival

Bible Reading: **Psalms 85:6**
Wilt thou not revive us again: that thy people may rejoice in thee?

Beloved at some points in our christian race we need to retreat to be revived, revitalised and to reinforce and gather more power and strength to move ahead. We should constantly examine our lives, we should from time to time take a check on our lives to know how much we have done for the Lord and how much we need to put in more or whether we need a change and a revival in any aspect of our christian lives.

Beloved, we need a revival and a change when we are not baptised with the Holy Ghost, when we do not know the word of God, when we are not interested in studying the word of God, when we do not have the knowledge of the word of God to use to resist the devil and when we are not working for God. We need revival when our service is unto men and not unto God, when we are not using our substances to support the work of God, when we are not giving to please God but men, when we are struggling to live right and when we easily or willingly fall into sin. We also need revival when we refuse to repent of all our sins.

According to the scriptures, revival brings rejoicing. It brings about recovery of lost joy, peace, health, glory, finance and so on. It puts you back on track with God and it brings back lost God's glory, His presence and the blessings.

Beloved, have you taken a check and you need revival? Hunger for it, ask for it and you shall receive it and the Lord of revival shall make you rejoice again.

NUGGET 67 - God Of Jacob Is Our Refuge

Bible Reading: **Psalms 46:6 -7**
The heathen raged, the kingdoms were moved. He uttered His voice, the earth melted.

Beloved no matter what is going on around us and around the world, be it rioting, political instability, Brexit, Boko Haram, Fulani herdsmen's attacks or any other form of terrorism or economic instability, we have a Heavenly Father who is the greater power, greater than the greatest powers and greater than any problem. He has been and will always be with us therefore we shall not fear.

The scriptures said that that God who is the Lord of hosts is with us and the God of Jacob is our refuge and our strength. Presidents, leaders, friends, brothers and sisters may fail but our God is eternally powerful. So do not let yourself fall into despair and be troubled when uncertainty abounds, seek God for strength, refuge and confidence in your circumstances and tell Him to provide comfort and relief from your anxieties and worries and He will.

NUGGET 68 - No Condemnation

Bible Reading: **Romans 8:1**
There is therefore now no condemnation to them which are in Christ Jesus, who walk not after the flesh but after the spirit.

Beloved, it is very important we know that the devil is a great accuser and that all he does day in and day out is to find faults to present to God against His children. He is very good at sending the spirit of condemnation to the children of God to make them loose confidence and fellowship with God.

The devil makes you feel bad even when you have not sinned against God and he makes you feel even worse when you have obtained forgiveness for the sins you committed long before you even came to Christ.

The devil uses condemnation to rob the children of God their miracles, due blessings, rights and benefits from God. Condemnation from the devil brings down your faith and your worthiness before God. It comes up first whenever you want to pray just to make you feel unworthy to go boldly before the throne of God to obtain mercy and once you are unable to pray, the devil will have the upper hand in your life and do as he desires.

Beloved I want you to know that there is no form of condemnation for any one who is in Christ, who has given his life wholeheartedly to Christ, who now walks and is led by the spirit of God. Do not let any devil condemn you and be quick to remind the devil that you are not condemned whenever he comes condemning you in your spirit.

NUGGET 69 - Mortify The Deeds Of The Body

Bible Reading: **Romans 8:13**
For if ye live after the flesh, you shall die: but if ye through the Spirit do mortify the deeds of the body ye shall live.

Beloved, there is a constant war between the flesh and the spirit and if the flesh wins it takes over a man and if the spirit wins, the spirit takes over. It is worthy to note that the flesh profits nothing and according to the scriptures, allowing flesh to take over brings nothing but death but the spirit gives life.

Do not live in the flesh so you will not fulfil the lust thereof. Flesh is a temporary accommodation, the flesh does not want to go to heaven, the flesh is the enemy of the spirit and enemy of God too; It produces sins. Flesh invites and opens doors to devil's attacks if we fulfil its desires. Living in the flesh brings about eternal damnation which is hell fire and satisfying the flesh puts the spirit in danger of death. Obeying the flesh which has a short lifespan puts man in all manner of troubles so it is better not to obey the flesh to avoid the consequences.

Beloved, there is no greater wisdom than crucifying and mortifying the flesh to give your soul an eternal life for what shall it profit a man to gain the whole world and loose his soul. Living in the flesh, satisfying the fleshy desires profits absolutely nothing. On the other hand, walking in the spirit and living in the spirit promises eternal life which is our ultimate goal in life. Obey the voice of God and His commands and the flesh will not have dominion over you and you shall not produce the fruits of the flesh but the fruits of the spirit.

It might not be an easy task to mortify the flesh but with the help of the Holy Spirit all things are possible.

NUGGET 70 - Be Persistent!

Bible Reading: **Colossians 4:2**
Continue in prayer and watch in the same with thanksgiving.

Beloved there is power in persistency. Jesus in Luke 18:3, through the parable of the widow and the unjust judge established the fact that there is power in persistent prayer. That scripture narrated a parable of a widow who constantly went to a Judge seeking of him to avenge her of her adversary even when she was not getting attention or answers she kept on going and going until the Judge decided to answer her less she wearied him. This parable simply illustrated the power of consistency and persistency in prayer even though the answers seem not to be coming.

In 2Kings 5, Naaman was asked by Prophet Elisha to deep himself seven times into River Jordan before he could be healed. Imagine what would have happened if Naaman had given up at the sixth deep into the River; he would not have been healed and his miracle was just around the corner at the next deep.

So many of us give up just when our miracle is about to come, just when a little more prayer or push would have landed us there or would have released the Angel of our blessings.

In 1st King 18, Elijah prayed for the rain seven times, also sent his servant seven times to go and see if the prayer had been answered by rain coming down but only at the seventh time did his servant see only a tiny sign not even the real rain and Elijah quickly released his faith and asked the servant to go and announce the coming of the rain. Sometimes we pray severally and we see a little sign that God could be answering us, we need to grab that sign and apply faith and call forth the full results of our prayers.

Some prayers may not be answered immediately, some may and some need fasting to be added but the bottom line is to pray until results come. Do not give up too easily or say "I have prayed and prayed and God is not answering and is happening". Some demons are very stubborn and persistent so you too need to be stubborn and persistent to match and conquer them.

Develop the attitude of "I will never give up until I get result." Pray until something happens. The scripture says "continue in prayer with thanksgiving" and you shall get results.

CHAPTER 8

Nugget 71
God Understands

Nugget 72
Best Ways To Deal With Your Enemies.

Nugget 73
Best Ways To Deal With Your Enemies II

Nugget 74
Best Ways To Deal With Your Enemies III

Nugget 75
The Power Of Prayer

Nugget 76
The Word Of God Is Life And Health

Nugget 77
Wrestle With The Angel Of Your Blessings

Nugget 78
Lest By Any Means, I Myself Should Be A Cast Away

Nugget 79
You Are Like Mount Zion Which Cannot Be Removed

Nugget 80
But I Come to Thee in The Name of The Lord of Hosts

NUGGET 71 - God Understands

Bible Reading: **Hebrews 2:16 & 18**
For verily He took not on Him the nature of angels; but He took on Him the seed of Abraham.
For in that He Himself hath suffered being tempted, He is able to succour them that are tempted.

Jesus took the form of man, He tasted death, sickness, poverty, lack etc. I am sure when He was about to die on the cross he suffered seizures, headaches due to the thorns on His head, body pains because of the beatings, anaemia because of the too much blood that flowed out of His wounds, He had weakness and poor vision due to the wounds around His eyes, He was booed and He was shamed even before His death, He was tempted by the devil himself. The sufferings were so much that He begged His father to take them away if possible.

Beloved, He suffered in a great manner, He himself has been there, He understands exactly what you are going through, the scripture says He is not an High Priest who cannot be touched with the feelings of our infirmities (Hebrews 4:15) If He feels your pains so why can't He help you. The only problem is sin which prevents Him from helping and unbelief too, if we can get rid of those, He will help us.

NUGGET 72 - Best Ways To Deal With Your Enemies I

Bible Reading: **Ephesians 6: 11**
Put on the whole armour of God that you may be able to stand against the wiles of the devil.

There is a constant war between the powers of darkness, invisible enemies, spiritual wickedness in heavenly places and the children of God. This war is not a physical one; it does not involve physical strength and weapons. The scripture says that the weapons of our war are not canal.

Beloved once you decamp from the devil's kingdom into the kingdom of Christ Jesus by accepting Him as your Lord and saviour, you get the devil infuriated and you become his number one enemy for life and a war begins. You can only defeat the devil and win this particular war by not only accepting Christ as your saviour but by developing a personal relationship with Him. You develop a personal relationship with Jesus by getting closer to Him, making Him your friend and talking to Him always. Learn to do nothing without consulting Him first. Learn to study the word of God frequently and obey the commandments therein. Learn to sin in order not to off end Him and by so doing, you will be able to win the war because the only person the powers of darkness and the devil their master respect and fear is Jesus, the only one who can help you win the enemy.

Also covet and embrace the person of the Holy Spirit. Listen to Him and always ask for His assistance in anything. The Holy Spirit helps you in this war. He is the third person in the trinity assigned to help you in your christian journey and in this warfare. If you do not have Him, desire Him and ask for Him and He will come to you.

NUGGET 73 - Best Ways To Deal With Your Enemies II

Bible Reading: **Romans 12:20**
Therefore if thy enemy hunger, feed him; if he is thirst give him drink: for in so doing thou shalt heap coals of fire on his head.

Beloved, enemies abound but the grace of God abounds even much more. We cannot rule away the fact that there are enemies, enemies of our souls, enemies of the kingdom, enemies of our body but God has given us power over them and the scriptures has outlined how to deal with them especially the physical enemies.

One of the ways to deal with your enemies according to our the scriptures is to feed them if they are hungry and give them water to drink if they are thirsty. Romans 12:20 simply means that you should be nice to your enemies. Your enemies naturally would want you to go hungry, go broke or even want you dead or that evil should befall you but do not retaliate or wish them ill. It is a very difficult thing to do but that is the way to deal with your enemies. The scripture said that by so doing, you shall heap coals of fire on their heads. Coals of fire could be God's punishment on them, it could be their own evil plans against you returning back to them and it could your desires on them.

In Mathew 5:44, the word of God said that you should love your enemies, bless them that curse you, do good to them that hate you and pray for them who despitefully use you and persecute you. Another way of dealing with our enemies is to love them even when their hatred reaches the sky, bless them even when all they do mornings, evenings and nights is to curse you, bless them anyways for whomsoever God has blessed no one can ever curse. Their curses will never be of any eff ect because you have blessed them for whatever a man sows he reaps. If you bless them you will reap blessings and if they continue to curse you they will continue to reap curses.

Yet another way to deal with your enemies is to cry unto God concerning them and report them to God even though God knows them and knows what they have done or are doing to you. Psalms 56:9 said that when you cry unto God, then your enemies shall turn back for God is for you.

Beloved do not fret over your numerous enemies. Just be nice to them, bless them, pray for them but cry unto God also making sure you in right standing with God to please Him and He will make your enemies your footstool.

NUGGET 74 - Best Ways To Deal With Your Enemies III

Bible Reading: **Isaiah 54:14b**
...for thou shalt be far from operation: for thou shalt not fear..

Fear is a weapon of the enemy. The scriptures said that fear is a torment and torment is an operation and for you to be far from operation you have to remove fear. Before the enemy could defeat you, he will first of all instill fear in you then gain his victory over you. The devil plans his victory by instilling fear because he knows that with fear he crumbles your defence, with fear he pulls down your faith and your confidence in God. So beloved, another way of dealing with and defeating the enemy is by eroding fear completely from your life.

The enemy uses fear to ensnare and hold captive his victims. He uses fear to gain legal grounds to afflict and oppress. Remember the Psalmist in Psalms 23:4 and be confident that even though you walk through the valley of shadow of death, the Lord is with you and will deliver you only if you fear not. Beloved, it is true that God is with us and that should give us confidence enough to face the enemy squarely no matter what he brings.

We wrestle not against flesh and blood but against powerful powers. These powers are so powerful that when they start their operations, terror and fear seem to be inevitable but if only we can disallow that fear from gripping us and see the hand of God instead and letting the knowledge that God can never leave nor abandon His own sink inside of us. The knowledge that our God is much more powerful than those powers will erase fear automatically and completely and obtain our desired victory over our enemies.

Beloved do never entertain fear. The name of Jesus, the blood of Jesus and the word of God are available for us to use against the enemy for with God we can never be defeated.

NUGGET 75 - The Power Of Prayer

Bible Reading: **James 5:16b**
The effectual fervent prayer of a righteous man availeth much.

Beloved, it is through prayer we communicate with God and tell Him all of our problems. He is our father and He is bound by a father child relationship to hear and answer us and take care of our problems but in order to get Him to hear and answer us, we need to please Him. We need to examine the scriptures and find out what He requires from us so that our prayers will be powerful and effective enough to break chains and give us deliverance.

The scriptures says that a prayer must be effectual which means that it must be capable of producing what we desired from God. If you pray and nothing happens or you are not getting the desired answer, you must ask yourself certain questions. You must reexamine yourself whether you are praying the right prayer or praying the will of God and most importantly whether your ways are right before God.

The power of your prayer is dependent on the power of your purity and sanctity. The word of God says that the prayer of a sinner is an abomination before God and that His hands are not short nor His ears deaf that He cannot hear us but our sins form a separation between Him and us.

The scriptures also talked about the fervency of prayer. Prayer should be done with absolute concentration, pouring out of mind with intense emotions. Most times when we pray, our minds wander from place to place, from one thing to another and at the end God cannot hear us nor pinpoint what we really need though He understands us but He needs us to concentrate and focus on Him while talking to Him. Imagine you talking to your Supervisor and you are not coherent because your mind is not on what you are saying.

Your Supervisor will not be able to make sense out of your discussion.

Beloved, most importantly we need to be righteous, clean-handed, just, upright and innocent of sins when we come to Him in prayer. We need to come with repentant heart asking for the forgiveness of our sins and not claiming righteous when we know we are not.

When we try all these, our prayers will be powerful and accepted before Him. He will show us mercy and answer us.

NUGGET 76 - The Word Of God Is Life And Health

Bible Reading: **Proverbs 4:20 -22**
My son, attend to my words; incline thine ear to my sayings.
Let them not depart from thine eyes; keep them in the midst of thine heart.
For they are life unto those that find them, and health to all their flesh.

Beloved health is in the word of God and life too is in the word of God. Proverbs 4:20-22 instruct us on how.

1. Attend to the word of God by studying and finding out what the word of God says in every situation you find yourself in and that will give you peace that will keep you healthy.

2. Develop the attitude of hearing the word of God by attending gatherings where the word of God is preached. Listening to sound teachings from true men of God will help you in time of need, set you free from anxiety, calm you down even in worst circumstances and keep you happy and healthy.

3. Meditate on the word of God to guide your steps not to make mistakes that could cost you your life and health. Meditation on the word keeps you from sin and helps you confront circumstances including that of your health.

The word of God you meditate on will give you a healthy heart because it gives peace of mind when you know that the word of God that you know and speak, will work for you in time of need.

NUGGET 77 - Wrestle With The Angel Of Your Blessings

Bible Reading: **Genesis 32:24 -26**
And Jacob was left alone; and there wrestled a man with him until the breaking of the day.
And when he saw that he prevailed not against him; and he touched the hollow of his thigh; and the hollow of Jacob's thigh was out of joint, as he wrestled with him.
And he said, let me go for the day breaketh. And he said, I will not let thee go, except thou bless me.

Beloved, there are blessings that would not come unless you fight and wrestle. There are some breakthroughs you will never have except you wrestle with the one who has the breakthroughs.

Jacob was able to get a name change by wrestling with the angel of his blessings. He was persistent, never giving up even when the angel touched the hollow of his joint and dislocated it he did not care about the pain but continued to wrestle. If Jacob had given up at the point his joint was dislocated he would not have gotten his blessings. He would not have gotten the change he so needed.

Many of us give up when the battle is at its highest and that is the point at which blessings are being released and at that point, God requires us to put in a little more input, a little more persistence and a little more faith.

Beloved, let us therefore learn from the scriptures and develop the spirit of 'I will never let go, I will never stop praying, I will never stop having faith, I will never stop believing God until I see my blessings come through, until I see my breakthroughs in my hands.'

NUGGET 78 - Lest By Any Means, I Myself Should Be A Cast Away

Bible Reading: **1st Corinthians 9:27**
But I keep under my body and bring it into subjection: lest by any means, when I have preached to others, I myself should be a cast away.

Beloved, it is very important that we constantly examine ourselves to know if we are going the right way and if we are doing well in our christian lives. A merchant takes stock at a particular time, some end of the year and some end of the month to know whether they are making profit or not and then make the necessary adjustments where needed to cob losses and make profits. So should we children of God do in our kingdom businesses and pursuit.

We are to take stocks of our lives. We are supposed to carry out a kind of personal analysis or survey by recalling our past lives and comparing them with our present lives. We are to Ponder on how we started our christian journeys and examine whether we are still in faith or not. We need to examine how far we have grown in the Lord, whether we are recording increase or decline in growth. We need to evaluate how many souls we have won for Christ especially through our lifestyles.

1st Corinthians 9:27 admonished that we should not evangelise to people, make them candidates for heaven and then miss heaven. Brother Paul knew that it would be a really bad situation if he converted souls to Christ then be a cast away at the end. Let us therefore examine ourselves today, identify our weaknesses and work on them and let us not always forget that Christ is coming back soon and live a life that will guarantee us heaven at last.

NUGGET 79 - You Are As Mount Zion Which Cannot Be Removed

Bible Reading: **Psalms 125:1**
They that trust in God shall be as mount Zion which cannot be removed but abideth forever.

The scripture described those who put their trust in God as mount Zion and irremovable. This means that they remain unshaken, unperturbed, undisturbed and still in all circumstances simply because they trust their God to be able to deliver. It also means that if God has placed them in a high place, they can never be removed from that place of high to low. If God had given those who trust in Him health, they can never be unhealthy and if He had placed them in certain positions, they can never be moved and if He had blessed them, no one can curse them.

The Lord delights in those who trust Him. He can do all it takes to see that they keep trusting Him and rely on Him solely. Trusting God comes from the knowledge of His word and who He is. If you know from His word that He cannot lie then that knowledge assures you that no matter what He truly cannot lie and must come through for you so you trust Him. If God has made some promises in His word concerning any situation in life then when such situation arises, knowing that God will make do His promises shows that you trust Him.pronounced you blessed because you have been tested and approved by Him that you trust.

Beloved it is good to just trust in God and be as that mountain that can never be removed from blessings to curses, from riches to poverty, from high positions to low, from good job to bad job, from greatness to lowness or from plenty to lack no matter the power of the enemy involved. No matter the strength of the enemies and no matter their positions in the kingdom of darkness, you will remain the king the lord has made you and will remain where the lord has placed you. Even if the enemy tries to move or remove you, he will never succeed as the scriptures had said, they shall fight but they shall not prevail. It is what it is.

NUGGET 80 - But I Come to Thee in The Name of The Lord of Hosts

Bible Reading: **1st Samuel 17:45**
Then said David to the Philistine, thou comest to me with a sword and with a spear and with a shield: but I come to thee in the name of the Lord of hosts, the God of the armies of Israel whom thou hast defiled.

Psalms 118:10
All nations compassed me about but in the name of the Lord will I destroy them.

There are situations that you know that it is only God that can save you. The kind that David faced with Goliath.

Beloved, who do you trust or remember when Goliath-like situations confront you; who do you go to war with? Do you go to war with your sword, your strength, your power, your might, your intelligence, your beauty, your wittiness, all your human armour or do you go war with the name of Jesus? Remember that the arms of flesh may fail but the name of Jesus never fails. It is not by power now by might but by the name of our Lord Jesus Christ. It is far better to go with to war with the name of Jesus.

The Psalmist said some trust in chariots and some in horses but we will remember the name of the Lord our God. What do you remember at first instance and you immediately when the enemy threatens? Do you remember Charms, Uncles or friends; all of them can fail. When someone threatens to deal with you; when situations and sickness threaten you, it is important you remember God and tell him.

Another thing to do when Goliath-like situations confront you is to do exactly what David did. David was bold enough to say to the raging Goliath "I know you are strong, I know you have powers, I know you have amours but I come against you in the name that is above your name, your powers, your strength and your weapons, the name of Jesus. David would not have come against Goliath if he did not know the name of the Lord or which word to speak and that is why it is important to get yourself acquainted with the word of God so you will be fully armed with the right weapon to confront your enemy.

The Psalmist further reconfirmed in Psalms 118:10 that the only thing we should go to war with is the name of Jesus and the only person to remember in times of difficulties is Jesus. Do not rely on any other name. Just call Him and He will answer His name and every evil knee in your life shall bow.

CHAPTER 9

Nugget 81
Durable Riches And Honour Are With God

Nugget 82
Feed Yourself With The Word

Nugget 83
Deal With That Prince Of Persia

Nugget 84
True Worshippers Never Lack

Nugget 85
Increase In Wisdom And Stature

Nugget 86
There Is No Time

Nugget 87
Pray and Praise

Nugget 88
We Are Heirs Of The Father

Nugget 89
Decree A Thing And It Shall Be Established

Nugget 90
Encourage Yourself In The Lord

NUGGET 81 - Durable Riches And Honour Are With God

Bible Reading: **Proverb 8:17 -18 & 21**
I love them that love me and those that seek me early shall find me. Riches and honour are with me, yea, durable riches and righteousness. That I may cause those that love me to inherit substance, and I will fill their treasures.

Beloved, good, durable riches, money and honour come from God but the reverse is the case for any wealth and honour that come from the devil. They do not last and they are cursed riches. God gives freely and His conditions are not wicked and unclear. The devil gives and gives dangerous conditions; conditions that you will later regret and make you unable to enjoy the wealth and honour he had given you.

Proverbs 8:21 explained that the condition that God requires from us to receive wealth, riches and honour is just to love Him. Most of us are not wealthy and not honored simply because we do not love God deeply from our heart of hearts. God declared that He loves those that love Him and that if they seek Him for anything including riches He would give them. If anybody you truly love ask you for anything especially those things that will better their lives you would give them if you have, so also God. He said that He would cause those that love Him to inherit substances and He would fill their treasures. This simply means that God will make you wealthy if you truly love Him. You might not be stupendously wealthy but you will never lack anything good including good health which is wealth too and this is because He is a moderate and good God and would not want to give you anything that would cause you to forget Him, keep you away from Him or deviate from Him.

Beloved, let us love God and begin to enjoy good wealth in every sense of it and remember to love Him sincerely not just by mere words for He knows those who truly loves Him.

NUGGET 82 - Feed Yourself With The Word

Bible Reading: **Joshua 1:8**
This book of the law shall not depart out of thy mouth; but thou shall meditate therein day and night, that thou mayest observe to do according to all that is written therein: for then thou shalt make thy way prosperous, and then thou shalt have good.

As the body cannot function very well without daily intake of well balanced diet so will our souls not be nourished and godly living not achieved without spiritual food which is the word of God. The word of God is to the soul what food is to the body. If you starve yourself of food, it will quickly show on your body and in no time people will start asking if you are unwell. It is also same when you do not read, study, meditate and apply the word of God to your life; it would not take time for backsliding to set in and before you know it, compromises will set in too and you start enjoying sin and loose your soul.

Beloved, if you are to become a strong Christian, you have to nourish your soul through reading and studying the word of God daily. A strong christian is one who is through the knowledge of the word of God able to withstand strong winds of temptations, evil arrows and their likes that the devil always brings. Remember that the word of God you know is the one you will use in time of adversity. A strong Christian is one who is living right and godly even in this world full of sin.

Apart from developing into a strong christian, the word of God will make your ways prosperous both spiritually, physically and materially. Again you shall have good and not bad success. Beloved are you looking for prosperity and good success? Go to the word of God, there you will find good guidance and wisdom to prosper and be successful in all that you do including prosperity in your christian life.

NUGGET 83 - Deal With That Prince Of Persia

Bible Reading: **Daniel 10:13a**
But the prince of the kingdom of Persia withstood me one and twenty days..

Beloved, most of our prayers and request receive answers. Most often when we inquire of God of our answers, He would confirm that He had already given us what we requested. Whenever such is the case, just know that there is a prince of Persia withholding your answers.

First we need to check and identify that prince of Persia and deal with it. Prince of Persia could be our sins for His hands are not short to save us nor His ears deafened that He cannot hear and answer us but our sins do separate us from Him and answers to our prayers. All we have to do in this case is to acknowledge our sins, confess and forsake them and God will have mercy and release our answers.

Again the prince of Persia could be demons released by the devil to withhold our answers. At times we have no known and unconfessed sins just that powers that be, wicked powers and agents of darkness do not want God to be glorified in our lives and they conspire to withhold our answers so we can curse God and deny Him just like in the case of Job. All we have to do is to remain steadfast and faithful to God and hand them over to God and God is bound to defend His name and release our answers and we will be like Job whose later end became better than his beginnings.

Another prince of Persia could be our attitude to prayers. Sometimes our attitude to prayer, that is the way we present our request to God hinders our answers; most times we ask amiss as in James 4:3 or asking with the wrong motives. Only if we can correct such and ask correctly and according to His will, then our answers can come.

Prince of Persia could be lack of faith too. Lack of faith can hinder our answers because the scripture says without faith it is impossible to receive answers. So beloved, let us deal with those Prince of Persias and God will spur His Angel to action to get and deliver our answers to us.

NUGGET 84 - True Worshippers Never Lack

Bible Reading: **Psalms 67:5 -7**
Let the people praise thee O God: let all the people praise thee.
Then shall the earth yield her increase, and God even our own God shall bless us
God shall bless us and all the ends of the earth shall fear Him.

Beloved, true worshippers or they that worship God in truth and in spirit never lack. The Psalmist said so in Psalms 37:25 that the righteous can never be forsaken and can never beg for bread. The Psalmist used the word 'never' which means it has never happened neither will it ever happen that any seed born of God will beg for bread. The bread referred to here is food and it can also be anything good that we desire.

God never ever forsakes His people especially the ones who praise Him day in and day out, those who worship Him in truth and in spirit and those who sincerely pour out their spirits to Him. According to the scriptures, God always causes an increase in His worshippers lives whenever they worship. He causes His blessings to flow from heavens to the earth upon His worshippers.

He makes them to lie down in green pastures and restores their souls. He makes them flourish like the tree planted by the riverside. He never ever withholds anything good from them. He causes them to arise and shine. He gives them plenty even in the midst of famine.

He delivers them from all troubles and set their feet on Jesus the rock and puts a new song in their mouths and never allowed them to lack.

So please beloved, if you are not in the category of the true worshippers of God, make an amend and join the true worshippers' wagon and worship Him. Give Him quality praise and worship due to Him and serve Him in truth and in spirit with all your might, body and soul including your time and substances and watch Him bless and increase you.

NUGGET 85 - Increase In Wisdom And Stature

Bible Reading: Luke 2:52
And Jesus increased in wisdom and stature, and in favour with God and man.

Beloved, we are Christ and Christ is us the very day we gave our lives to Him and professed Him as our Lord and personal saviour. We are everything He was on earth.

He experienced growth in every aspect of His life therefore we too are to grow spiritually. we are not to remain stagnant, we are to receive the necessary nutrients we need from God's word to grow into strong trees and plants. Strong trees and plants are well rooted if they get sufficient nutrients from the soil. They are able to withstand adverse weather conditions and they bear good fruits. Beloved, the fruits we are supposed to bear are mentioned in Galatians 5:22& 23 which are Love, joy, peace, long-suffering, gentleness, goodness, faith, meekness and temperance. Jesus all that on earth.

The scripture explains that Jesus grew in wisdom and stature. It is the will and desire of our father that we grow even in our Christian faith. Hebrew 6:1 said that we should leave the elementary teachings of Christ and grow unto maturity. God expects us to progressively increase in our knowledge of Him on daily basis. He wants us to experience Him in broader and newer way everyday and the word of God is the source of that growth. If we do not get nourished by His words we do not grow and if we do not grow we cannot bear fruits. A tree stunted in growth will not be able to mature enough to bear fruits.

Beloved, what God requires of us is to love, serve and be in constant fellowship with Him through communion with Him in prayers and the study of His words;. He requires us to grow in Him and bear fruits of righteousness which will enable us obtain His promises and our inheritance in Him.

NUGGET 86 - There Is No Time

Bible Reading: John 9:4
I must work the work of Him that sent me while it is day; the night cometh when no man can work.

Beloved time is running out. There is no time to waste any more. We might be thinking that Christ has lingered in His coming. This is a wrong thinking that the devil uses to make us less prepared and not ready for heaven. It has also affected the task of soul winning that God had commissioned into our hands.

From the passage of the scriptures, John 9:4, we can see the eagerness and the urgency in the voice of Jesus when He made that statement. He knew He had to do the work of His father urgently because He had no time and no room to give to the devil to take those whom God has given Him. He has to cover all areas before the devil does.

"The night cometh when no man can work work" used by Jesus in the scripture has several meanings. It could mean when one could be stricken with age and one can no longer do much work for the kingdom due to age related issues and weakness. It can also mean our Lord Jesus appearing suddenly and there would be no time to do any work for the kingdom. It could also mean natural rapture which is the physical death which is appointed unto every man on earth and the time is hidden from all mankind.

Beloved, let us therefore awake from our spiritual slumber. Let us stop procrastinating for the time to do the work of Him that sent us is now. The time to tell that someone about Christ is now. it is time to carry our bibles and hit the streets and make disciples of Christ. We are saved to save others; do not be selfish and enjoy the goodness of God alone, let someone know that knowing and serving God is the only thing that matters. The devil is busy making disciples, turning the whole world to his side; child of God do not let him take over the world for Christ will soon come back again.

NUGGET 87 - Pray and Praise

Bible Reading: **Acts 16:25-26**
And at midnight Paul and Silas prayed, and sang praises unto God, and the prisoners heard them.
And suddenly there was an earthquake, so that foundations of the prison were shaken: and immediately all the doors were opened and everyone's bands were loose.

Beloved prayer is good but when we add it with praise, it works wonders. Let us look closely at the scriptures and derive some lessons that will help us a lot if we apply them.

First, the scripture said 'at midnight' Paul and Silas prayed and sang praises unto God. This shows that there is an important and significant hour for prayer and praise that can get the type of results that Brother Paul and Silas got. Most of the activities of the powers of darkness are usually carried out at midnight hours also God's power is made more available for all who seeks Him at those hours to counter those forces of darkness.

Our text also stated that Paul and Silas prayed and praised, these two great men of God knew the importance of prayer and praise; they knew that the situation they were in required them not only to pray but to back their prayer up with a powerful weapon which is praise. Beloved know it now that praise is a powerful spiritual weapon. From the scriptures, Paul and Silas praises were violent and loud that was why other prisoners heard them and that is why it is important for us to sing out aloud, to be heard.

Lastly from our scriptures we can see the results of prayer and praises. The scripture said 'suddenly'... which means that prayer and praises can bring sudden results. The scripture also recorded that there was an earthquake, shakings of the prisons foundations, and immediately doors were opened and everyone's bands were removed.

Beloved there is power in prayer and praise. When we pray and add praise, we might not see buildings shaking and earthquakes but spiritually there is earthquake in the kingdom of darkness, evil foundations are destroyed, there are great open doors, chains, bands and barriers are broken, freedom buttons are activated, deliverance and healing takes place.

NUGGET 88 - We Are Heirs Of The Father

Bible Reading: **Romans 8:17**
And if children, then heirs; heirs of God, and joint-heirs with Christ; if so be that we suffer with Him, that we may be also glorified together.

Beloved, according to the above scripture, we are co heirs with Christ, obtaining the promises of the father, reigning with Him in glory, power and might and doing greater things than He did. An heir is one who by right is entitled to an inheritance. Jesus is the heir of His father and by virtue of our salvation through His blood we are made heirs of the father too. As many as receive Him they are sons of God and if we be sons then we are His seed and heirs to the promises and inheritance of God who is our father.

We are one with Christ, we are in Christ and Christ is in us. If Christ therefore is in us we are to act like Him for as He is so are we in this world(1st John 4:17) and greater works He did through the father we shall do also.

Christ has the power to heal and if Christ is in us, that same power to heal is in us too. Christ has the power to do the impossible and that same power is in us too. Christ is meek and gentle, He possessed and manifested all the fruits of the spirit and we are to possess and manifest all the fruits of the spirit just like Him because He is in us.

Therefore beloved since we are born of God just as Christ is then what is true of Christ is true of us. Let us not limit ourselves anymore. Let us make full use of the power Christ has because that same power is in us and at work in us. If Christ is the head we have no business being at the tail. If Christ overcame the world, we cannot let the world defeat us. If Christ succeeded in His ministry, we cannot fail. If Christ casted out demons, we too can.

So beloved, go ahead and act, live and demonstrate the power you have as an heir over situations and demons.

NUGGET 89 - Decree A Thing And It Shall Be Established

Bible Reading: Job 22:28
Thou shalt also decree a thing and it shall be established unto thee and the light shall shine upon thy ways.

To decree is to decide with authority. Kings usually make decrees and when they do it becomes a rule and a law that must be obeyed. Decree carries power and authority. You cannot make decrees keeping quiet. You have to speak with your mouth. You can only pass a decree with your mouth. And what do you decree? You issue a decree of what you want or desire and when you do that, back it up with what God had decreed concerning you and whatever you have decreed shall be established.

The scriptures said that you shall decree a thing and it shall be established and the light of God will shine upon your ways. This verse of scripture simply means that decrees bring establishments and cause the light of God to shine upon your ways, your businesses, your careers, your homes, your families and anything at all that has to do with you.

Beloved anything you so desire simply give a decree that they come to you and whenever you are decreeing, do that with so much authority because that has been given to you by your father who owns everything. Also remember that you are a King and Kings make decrees that stand; so decree like a King too and it shall be established. Also any area of your life that is experiencing darkness, just pass a simple decree and the light of God will suddenly shine upon those areas and they will come alive.

NUGGET 90 - Encourage Yourself In The Lord

Bible Reading: **1st Samuel 30:6**
And David was greatly distressed; for the people spake of stoning him, because the soul of all the people was grieved, every man for his sons and for his daughters, but David encouraged himself in the Lord His God.

David though was depressed initially but did not continue in his sorrows, he did not go about telling people his problems to attract sympathy or pity, he did not consult other gods nor seek assistance from them, he did not just sit down and do nothing about the situation. The scripture above says he encouraged himself in the Lord.

Beloved, what do you do in extreme situations, what do you do when you have tried all that you know and yet the situation still refuses to improve, what do you do when you have prayed all the prayers you know how to pray and yet there seem to be no improvement on that situation. Just like David, encourage yourself in the Lord for if David could do it you too can do it.

You can encourage yourself in the Lord by letting the word of God you know to minister to your heart reassuring you that if God has said it, He will do. You can also encourage yourself by letting that word of God you know bring joy into your heart instead of worry. Remind God that His word said this and that concerning the situation and most importantly speak, confess and believe those words and you will see a change in that situation.

CHAPTER 10

Nugget 91
The Lord Saveth His Anointed

Nugget 92
You Are The Temple Of God

Nugget 93
Say It, Have It

Nugget 94
He Has Broken The Gates

Nugget 95
Increase In Wisdom And Stature

Nugget 96
We Are Ambassadors For Christ

Nugget 97
You Can Trust God

Nugget 98
The Good Problem

Nugget 99
Can God Boast About You To The Devil?

Nugget 100
Be Alert In The Spirit

NUGGET 91 - The Lord Saveth His Anointed

Bible Reading: **Psalms 20:6**
Now knoweth I That the Lord saveth His anointed, He will hear him from His holy heaven with the saving strength of His right hand.

Beloved God is our saviour, He is our saving grace. His eyes are always on us as long as we allow Him. He shields us from every harm both known and unknown.

David is a typical example of the anointed of God just like we are. He fought wars, he was pursued by deadly enemies even his best friend's father but in all, the Lord delivered him and saved him. That should give us the confidence that no matter how fierce the battle is and no matter who the enemy is, the Lord will always save His people and deliver them.

According to the scripture, He will save with His saving strength; He has a saving strength greater and more powerful than your problems or whatever force that is holding you down; His strength is usually perfected in our weaknesses, our sorrows and pains. He is ever ready to demonstrate His saving strength to all who needs it. His right hand is powerful and is exalted above our problems. His right hand fights our battles. His right hand is not only involved but His ears too; He hears us from His high heavens whenever we call to save us and deliver us.

The only problem is that most of His children trust in chariots, horses, their armours; most times they do not remember the name of the Lord which is very important because it is when you remember someone and call for help that help will come. The scripture says that it is when you do not trust in your armours and remember the name of the Lord your God that the Lord will come down and bring your enemies and your problems down and you will stand above them. Do call on Him and He will answer you.

NUGGET 92 - You Are The Temple Of God

Bible Reading: **1st Corinthians 6:19**
What? Know ye not that your body is the temple of the Holy Ghost which is in you, which ye have of God, ye are not your own.

A temple is a place for worship; a dwelling place. 1st Corinthians 6:19 said that you are the dwelling place of the Holy Spirit. You are therefore under obligation to take care of the dwelling place of the Holy Spirit which is your body. Taking care of your body involves both spiritual and physical exercises. The Holy Spirit does not and cannot dwell in a filthy environment. He desires us which are His temple to be clean both outwardly and inwardly. He desired us to be holy, according to Romans 12:1. which are to present our bodies as living sacrifices, holy and acceptable unto God. We are to flee from all that can pollute our bodies and render them unsuitable for the habitation of the Holy Spirit

We are to treat our body like a temple of God not just like flesh with blood and water flowing in it. It is important to note that our body and mind work together and for us to have a healthy mind, we must have healthy body that is why it is very vital to take care of the body in order to have a healthy mind which worships the Lord in truth and in spirit. To have a healthy body, we must exercise regularly and try not to over work the body. Over working the body makes it difficult to connect with the Holy Spirit, to pray and to attend church activities which helps in your spiritual growth.

Meditation on the word of God is another way of taking care of the body spiritually. 2nd Timothy 2:15 enjoined us to study the word of God always. Also Joshua 1:8 instructed us to meditate on the word of God day and night. The body is a place where God Himself dwells and must be taken care of. Simple exercises such as walking is one of the ways we can take care of the body. Stopping one stop before actual bus stops and walking the rest can also be of great help to the body. For the spiritual exercise, adopting an easy method of quick morning meditation on God's word before going out or quick meditation before sleep is key.

NUGGET 93 - Say It, Have It

Bible Reading: **Mark 11:23**
For verily I say unto you, that whosoever shall say unto this mountain, be thou removed and be thou cast into the sea; and shall not doubt in his heart, but shall believe that those things which he saith shall come to pass; he shall have whatever he saith.

Beloved, it is important to speak good, positive and productive words into our lives. A florist conducted an experiment. In the experiment, he planted two flowers in two different pots, with the same soil, light exposure, watering, air and manure and labeled them A and B. Every morning he says to flower A "you shall blossom and shine, you shall bear fruit and live". To flower B he says "you shall not produce, you shall not blossom, you shall not shine, you shall not live". After a long while the flower in pot A began to flourish, grow and blossom in to a beautiful flower but the flower in pot B began to turn to yellow, pale then brown and finally died.

The story above simply demonstrates the fact that there is power in spoken words. God Himself created the earth, the seas, the light and the animals with just His words. Mark 11:23 further confirmed that there is power in words. The principle of 'say it, have it' can be applied to call forth all the good desires of your hearts. It is very important that whenever you wake up, speak good into your day, your life, your family and back it up with prayers. Speak the word because whatever you want when you pray and believe you shall have them.

Most times we worry so much and into the night and when we wake up, we continue to worry and forget to do the needful. Forget about what is happening now, do not carry over worries; try to speak into a new day even if the day turns out bad still do not stop, continue to speak and when it shall come to pass, it will include all that you have spoken before.

NUGGET 94 - He Has Broken The Gates

Bible Reading: Psalms 107:16
For He has broken the gates of brass and cut the bars of iron in sunder.

A gate is a moveable barrier in a fence or wall. Gates are barriers, obstacles, hinderances and blockages set up by the devil to inhibit endeavours and destinies of men especially the children of God. The good news according to our definition of gates is that they are moveable. The fact that we know that gates are moveable will help us relax whenever we noticed that the devil has built a gate around either our jobs, careers, finances, families or children because the gates must definitely be moved.

The devil does not like us therefore he constantly build this gate of brass around anything that concerns us just to pull us away from God but we should be of good cheer because we have a freer, a remover of those gates, our Lord Jesus Christ. He came into the world to redeem men from the power of darkness. These gates cannot be locked up for long. The gates of brass cannot be so strong that the work of His redemption cannot break through it. They cannot too big for His blood to flow through and damage them.

There is no issue Jesus cannot handle and there is no hinderance that He cannot remove.

Psalms 107:16 said He has broken those gates of bras and went further to cut the bars of iron which represents the devil's prison which he uses to subdue and hinder us from achieving our destinies.

NUGGET 95 - Obedience Is Better Than Sacrifice

Bible Reading: 1st Samuel 15:22
And Samuel said, hath God as great delight in burnt offerings and sacrifices as obeying the voice of the Lord? Behold, to obey is better than sacrifice and to hearken than the fat of rams.

Jeremiah 7:23
But this thing commanded I them, saying, obey my voice and I will be your God, and ye shall be my people: and walk ye in all the ways that I have commanded you, that it may be well unto you.

God has been so good to us. He has given us almost if not all we asked of Him. Obedience is what He requires from us apart from praise. God does not require food from us, He does not require car or any other gift from us other than obedience to His commands. 1st Samuel 15:22 accounted that Saul obeyed the voice of the people rather than the voice of God and because of that God rejected him as king and chose another in his stead. This means that disobedience to God's commands can bring outright rejection from God.

Even when it seemed that Saul was doing God a favour by trying to offer Him good burnt offerings, God still did not accept that, this further shows that God does not want our offerings to replace our obedience to His instructions. Beloved, has God instructed you or laid it in your heart to do something for Him and you are quite convinced that it was God who spoke to you? Do not delay any longer in carrying out that instruction to avoid the consequences thereof.

Jeremiah 7:23 enumerated the gains in obeying God's command and instructions. Beloved, please note that the scripture said that if you obey God, He will be your God and do you know what it means for God to be your God? It means He will always be there for you doing all He is bound to do as 'your God' and that include fighting your battles, protecting you, defending you, providing for you and eternal life at last. Another gain is that you will be His and that is awesome; when you are His, it means He owns you and whatever He owns can never be destroyed nor stolen; the enemy will never destroy, kill or steal you. There is yet another gain and that is that it shall be well with you.

Therefore Beloved, choose to obey God today that it may be well with you.

NUGGET 96 - We Are Ambassadors For Christ

Bible Reading: 2nd Corinthians 5:20
Now then we are ambassadors for Christ, as though God did beseech you by us, we pray you in Christ's stead, be ye reconciled to God.

An Ambassador is one who represents and to represent is to take a place of someone and a representative is one who represents others. Beloved, we represent Christ and at the same time act as representatives of heaven. Christ came to earth sent by His Heavenly Father to do His works, to fulfill a particular mission which is to save mankind. During His earthly works He represented His father well both in character and in works. He did exactly what the father asked Him to do and was His father personified. And when He finished His works He handed over to His disciples and us to represent Him.

Beloved how well are you representing Christ, God cannot come down from heaven to speak to sinners about salvation of their souls, He needs people like you and I to do that even though He does the conversion Himself. God cannot come down from heaven to feed the hungry like He did in the wilderness; He needs us to do that for Him. Sometimes what the unbelievers need is not the words that we speak to them on repentance but our actions, deeds, behaviours, kindness, godly characters and genuine love.

Christ was able to convert many unto Himself due to His actions, He showed love even to the most sinful men and women. He conducted Himself in the manner that is worthy of note even when He was falsely accused and sentenced to death. He was full of mercy, compassion and was very forgiving when He was on earth. How do we handle our accusers, those who hurt us and those who do not share same values and beliefs with us? How do we treat people generally both rich and poor. Jesus represented God well in these capacities. God expects us as good representatives of Him to act likewise. All we need is His grace for we cannot do anything without His grace. Constantly ask for His grace and He will make it available.

NUGGET 97 - You Can Trust God

Bible Reading: **Proverb 3:5 -6**
Trust in the Lord with all thine heart and lean not unto thine own understanding.
In all thy ways acknowledge Him and He shall direct thy paths.
Trust in the lord with all your heart and lean not on your own understanding.
In all your ways acknowledge Him and He shall direct your path.

Beloved, the above scripture is very true and very simple to understand. First it says trust in the Lord. Trust means have faith or confidence in, it means allow without fear, it means be confident about something, it also means expect and wish.

In our context it means have faith and confidence in God, allow God to take control, do not fear, be confident that God will and must do it, expect that God will do it or is doing it and expect results already.

Another part of that scripture said trust God with all your heart, not half of your heart. This means do not doubt and have strong faith. The scripture further said 'lean not on your own understanding', and it means do not depend on your own thinking, your feelings, your emotions or what you are seeing; do not think on how terrible the situation is and how impossible it is to be fixed. Just trust God that it will be fixed.

Finally, the scripture said 'in all your ways acknowledge God' which means in everything you do whether it is business, career, family, finance, health matters commit it to Him, acknowledge Him first and He will direct the way that matter will go.

Beloved, if God has said it, go to bed, it is done. The joy is supernatural that comes from knowing that you know that no matter the way things are, no matter what it is, God says "trust me" and truly all it takes is just to trust Him and it is finished. Years does not intimidate God. If you trust God, you will know how to be joyful in that situation and if you know how to be joyful in that situation, you will know how to wait upon the Lord and your answers must come.

NUGGET 98 - Good Problem

Bible Reading: **Romans 8:28**
And we know that all things work together for good to them that loves God, to them who are the called according to purpose.

Problems are not good neither are they pleasant but there are problems that are good and specially designed by the Omniscient God to set those He loves and those who love Him to the path of their destinies. God is a problem creator especially to those He has called according to purpose.

Beloved, all things work together for good to them that love God and to them that are called for a purpose. God has a purpose for our lives, if you are special, if you are uniquely unique; God's eyes are on you from conception and will direct your whole life and paths.

If you are a divine destiny and your destiny is tied to other destinies, there is always some mysteries around you. If there is a special purpose God wants you to fulfil, He usually allows some happenings your way. When such happens, most times prayer, fasting and crying to God do not make them go away. In such times, all you need is just to hold your peace and recognize that God is in it and it will not be long and you will understand why.

Take special note of that part of Romans 8:28 that said 'to them who are the called', all things work together for good for them. So beloved if you are having strange problems that refuse to go even after so much prayers just know that God could be the one because you are called for a purpose and when the time is due, you will know why and bless the name of the Lord for allowing you go through such.

NUGGET 99 - Can God Boast About You To The Devil?

Bible Reading: **Job 1:8**
And the Lord said unto Satan, hast thou considered my servant job, that there is none like him in the earth, a perfect and an upright man, one that feareth God and escheweth evil?

Beloved, God wants to be proud of us always. He always wants to look down from heaven at us and boast about us to the devil. He also wants to be able to tell the devil, the accuser of brethren that He knows us very well and that we cannot disappoint Him, betray Him or fall into temptations. He can even send the devil to go try us and see if can fall. But in most cases we disappoint Him by falling into the traps of the devil and the temptations that the devil brings.

Job was a child of God just like us. He feared and worshipped God just like us and it happened that when God boasted about him to the devil, the devil told God that job does not fear Him for nothing. This is exactly how he runs us down before God. The devil is always discussing us before God, telling Him we do not fear Him and that even if we fear Him, it is not for nothing. The devil tells God that we only worship Him because He gave us this and He gave us that. The devil usually proves this by attacking those blessings of God and most times we fail to recognise that and give in and start doubting God, His promises and His word and at extreme case we even fall out of faith entirely.

Beloved, let us learn from brother Job. God was proud of Job and boasted to the devil that He knew Job would never fall to his temptations even when the devil attacked all that God had blessed him with. Job was able to remain faithful and true to God refusing to curse and renounce God even when the pressure was to much to bear.

Beloved, let us remain faithful even in the face of extreme adversity, refuse to throw in the towel, refuse to listen to detrimental advice from the devil and those he uses, refuse to fall into sin or do anything that will make God loose His confidence in us and we end up loosing God's cover and heaven which is our ultimate goal. Job's later end was better than his beginning and that tells us that after we are tried and we win, we will always be better than we were and in all ramifications.

NUGGET 100 - Be Alert In The Spirit To Notice Your Divine Helper

Bible Reading: **2nd Kings 4:8 -17**
2nd Kings 4:17- And the woman conceived, and bare a son at that season that Elisha had said unto her, according to time of life.

Beloved, let us learn a few things from the woman of Shunem. For this woman to be recognised and mention in God's own written word, the Bible, it means her actions is very worthy of note and should be emulated.

Firstly, this woman was spiritually alert enough to notice Elisha, a great man of God who was always passing through her street. Please note that there are several other women and men who lived in that same street as the woman of Shunem who did not even noticed that Elisha passed by always not to talk of noticing how great a man of God he was. Had it been that the woman did not take time to notice Elisha may be she would remained barren for the rest of her life and would have died a barren woman. Most of us miss our divine helpers because we fail to notice them at the nick of time. Some of are not alert enough to notice them even when they are so close by.

Secondly, note that the woman had respect for the man of God. It is often said that the anointing you respect works for you and vice visa. She also made a special room for the man of God; indirectly she raised an alter in her house because the constant presence of the man of God automatically brought God's presence and blessing into her house. How many of us make room for God in our houses? We are supposed to carve out a place of prayer and worship not only in our hearts but in our houses too, this practice usually makes God dwell permanently in that place where you have set aside for Him. His presence never leaves there and His blessings that follow His presence will abound there too.

Also notice that God raised a voice for her in the person of Gehazi to tell the man of God what she needed at that time. Beloved, because this woman took care of a man of God, God raised a voice for her. We need to learn to take care of not only men of God but anybody at all God has positioned us to take care of and by so doing, God will open doors for us and pave ways for others to care for us.

CHAPTER 11

Nugget 101
The Set Time Has Come

Nugget 102
You Have Been Redeemed From Curses

Nugget 103
He Will Pardon

Nugget 104
Flee These Things

Nugget 105
And God Granted Him That Which He Requested

Nugget 106
Love And Not Hate

Nugget 107
Take No Thought

Nugget 108
Men Ought Always To Pray

Nugget 109
The Will Of God For You

Nugget 110
Always Be Joyful

NUGGET 101 - The Set Time Has Come

Bible Reading: **Psalms 102:13**
Thou shalt arise and have mercy upon Zion; for the time to favour her, yea the set time is come.

Beloved, we need favour especially God's favour. When mercy sets in, favour comes. Favour distinguishes a man. Mary attracted the favour of God. There were so many women who were virgins at the time of Mary but she caught divine attention which distinguished her. Favor makes a fool appear wise. Favour takes a man to the top. It is favour that makes a man thrive in harsh and unfavourable conditions in this world. Favour brings ordinary men before Kings and great men.

There is favour from men and there is favour from God. There is favour and there is high favour. Mary found not only favour but high favour from God.

Beloved, there is a set time for favour according to psalms 102:13. This means that things might first of all go wrong or be unfavourable and during this initial time of disfavour most of us do miss it through impatience. Some even try the fast lane because to them God is too slow but always remember that there is a waiting period and during this period, God expects us to trust Him, be full of faith, hope and expectations that He will surely arise and manifest His mercies and favour.

Set times vary from person to person so we do not have to bother ourselves when some people's set time comes and ours have not. One thing is very sure that no force, no human, no principality, no power, or demon can stop God when the set time comes to favour Zion.

NUGGET 102 - You Have Been Redeemed From Curses

Bible Reading: **Galatians 3:13**
Christ has redeemed us from the curse of the law being made a curse for us for it is written cursed is every one that hangeth upon a tree.

Beloved, curse is a very serious and powerful force that hinders an individual who labours under it. Curses are words backed up by evil spirits; It can drastically change a man's life and destiny for a life time if not lifted or broken.

Curses can be from men or from God, if a man curses you, you can be delivered by a higher force which is God but if God curses you, no man can deliver you that is why we should be very careful not to attract God's curses.

Some curses are genetic and in the DNA that is by virtue of birth and family, some curses are lawful, that is curses attracted by disobeying the word of God or the commandments of God. Things we know that are wrong and we still do them, they attract lawful curses and consequences.

There are unlawful curses which are curses we do not deserve but are pronounced by forces and powers of darkness. There are personal curses which are negative and evil words we pronounce on ourselves knowingly or unknowingly, and that is why we should be very careful of our utterances for our words carry power of fulfillment.

Beloved whichever curse it is, Christ has redeemed us from them all according to Galatians 3:13. The scriptures said He was made a curse which means that if we were cursed by someone or we attracted curses by virtue of our family lineage, Christ has been made that particular curse because He was hung on a tree and by hanging on a tree, He has taken away every curse under which we might be labouring. He has redeemed us with His blood from those curses. So beloved, for any curse at all you noticed that is operating in your life, use the scripture to demand your freedom and claim your blessings instead. Also remember you must be on the Lord's side and keep your hands clean and void of sin. He that comes to God should come with a clean plate so God can fill it up with blessings.

NUGGET 103 - He Will Pardon

Bible Reading: Isaiah 55:7
Let the wicked forsake his ways and the unrighteousness man his thoughts and return unto the Lord, and he will have mercy upon him and to our God, for He will abundantly pardon.

Beloved, it is the devil's desire that we loose our place in Christ. He is constantly bringing our ways, things that will make us fall but we are to be watchful of his plans and give him no place.

God is calling us first to constantly examine our lives inwardly to know if there is any wicked ways in us, forsake those ways and return to Him and He will have mercy on us, pardon us and accept us back to Himself.

The Psalmist practiced this constant examination in Psalms 139:23-24. He said search me O God and know my heart, try me and know my thoughts. And see if there is any wicked way in me and lead me in the way everlasting. This practice by David coupled with the fact that he knows how to praise God gained him great favour in the sight of God.

Let us emulate the Psalmist and constantly check ourselves to identify areas we are not measuring up to God's expectations, make amends and return to Him for He will abundantly pardon and receive us.

NUGGET 104 - Flee These Things

Bible Reading: **1st Timothy 6: 11**
But thou, O man of God, flee these things, and follow after righteousness, godliness, faith, love, patience, meekness.

Beloved, 1st Timothy 6:11 is referring to us. It is giving us a command to flee which means run away quickly, fly or take flight. When a command demands you to flee or run away quickly then there is danger if you do not obey that command. In this case the danger is sin and its consequences. Sin is dangerous and its consequences gravely.

Sin is an offence to God, it drives away His presence, it pollutes and hinders God from hearing prayers. It gives us away to the devil, it hinders prosperity, it prevents us from enjoying the promises of God, it crumbles the hedge of protection God builds around us and most importantly it denies us of inheriting the kingdom of God.

1st Cor 6:9-10 listed out some of the things God has commanded us to flee from which will keep us away from Him and from enjoying all the benefits of serving Him. Beloved, we are to be aware of sin and flee from them just as the scriptures advised because most of the problems we face today are as a result of sin and once sin is dealt with, majority of our problems are taken care of. The scripture further advised us to follow after righteousness, godliness, faith, patience, meekness and love which will lead us to heaven and make us enjoy God and all that He has promised us here on earth.

NUGGET 105 - And God Granted Him That Which He Requested

Bible Reading: 1st Chronicles 4:9-10
Jabez was more honourable than his brethren, and his mother called his name Jabez, saying because I bare him with sorrow.
And Jabez called the God of Jacob saying Oh that thou wouldest bless me indeed and enlarge my coast and that thy hand be with me, and that thou wouldest keep me from evil, that it may not grieve me. And God granted him that which he requested.

Beloved, let us learn a few lessons from these passages of the scriptures. Firstly, brother Jabez was cursed from birth, his mother indirectly cursed him from the name she gave to him according to the circumstances surrounding his birth. Most of us especially from Africa have links from idols because of our ancestor's involvements with them and this idolatry by our ancestors has had negative impacts on our lives and destinies. Let us learn from brother Jabez because though he was cursed from birth, the scripture said that he still was more honourable than his brothers. Why and how would someone who had been cursed from birth be better than those who were not. The answer is simple. Jabez did not call on any other God but the God of Abraham, Isaac and Jacob. he did not join any group that would make rich quickly. He did not allow the circumstances of his birth to hinder him. He refused to accept the negativities of life. and called on God, the one who formed him in his mother's womb, the one who has the key to his destiny and the one who had the final say in his life.

Therefore beloved, do not accept that curse of untimely death running in your family neither accept the fact that the family you come from are the 'never do wells' or that they rise and later fall or that there is a particular sickness or infirmity that runs in your family lineage or as they call it hereditary. Decide to call on God of Israel like Jabez did and God will answer you and change those circumstances just like He did for brother Jabez.

NUGGET 106 - Love And Not Hate

Bible Reading: James 2:8
If ye fulfil the royal law according to the scripture, thou shalt love thy neighbour as thyself, ye do well.

Beloved, James 2:8 is reminding us to love and not hate. The scriptures said you do well if you do love your neighbour and not hate. There are people who according to their attitudes and actions towards you, they do not deserve for you to love them at all but God instructed through His word that you should love them still. Some might have maltreated, abused and hated you but you should still have to show them love for God commanded so.

God commanded us to love our neighbour as our selves which means we should not only love but to love as we love ourselves too. This further means that you should love your neighbor the way you love yourself, you should treat your neighbor the way you treat yourself and you should not do to your neighbor what you do not want to be done to you. This is love without hypocrisy and the principle upon which relationships are built and maintained.

We do well if we manifest loving concerns for our neighbors as much as we do for ourselves. Neighbor here is referred to as everybody we come in contact with at any point in our lives with no exception of any person. We are to live the poor, rich, good, bad, young, old, lovable or not lovable. Showing love in respect of persons negates the commandments of God to love our neighbors as our selves. If we choose whom to love for the reasons of off ence, tribe, race or religion then we are manifesting partiality and hypocrisy which contradicts God, His commands and the principle laid by Him to love unconditionally just as He loved us.

Beloved, let us be guided to love and not hate no matter what.

NUGGET 107 - Take No Thought

Bible Reading: **Mathew 6:31**
Therefore take no thought, saying, what shall we eat? or what shall we drink? or where withal shall we be clothed?

Beloved, excessive worry and anxiety leads to depression, frustration and elevated blood pressure but why worry when the word of God said you should take no thought which means do not worry, do not bother, do not be anxious, do not stress, do not think. God, whom you are his knows exactly what you need and He knows you have issues that should be sorted out by Him.

Beloved, have you ever prayed and prayed through and suddenly a feeling of calmness overwhelms you and you have peace in your heart? That is exactly what God wants from you whenever you have a worrisome situation at hand. He does not want you to worry because He knows what that will bring. He knows that sickness, doubt and unbelief will come if worry and He would not want that for you. So instead of worrying, give Him thanks because thanksgiving is key.

Thanksgiving to God instead of worrying means you trust Him. It involves remembering what God did when you were in similar situation and giving Him thanks which makes you more confident that He will do it again. That confidence you have, kills worry. A heart full of thanks can never be sad at the same time. As you are thanking God, your heart is full of joy in anticipation of answered prayers. Thanking God as if He has answered your prayers challenges and spurs Him to action.

Therefore beloved, just table your issues before God through prayers and stop worrying. Worry can never solve a problem but prayer can.

NUGGET 108 - Men Ought Always To Pray

Bible Reading: **Luke 18:1**
And He spake a parable unto them to this end that men ought always to pray and not to faint.

Beloved the above scripture enjoined us to always pray and not faint. We should pray even more when answers are not forth coming. We can never over pray. Prayer is the weapon we have as Christ followers to war against the devil, our enemy. We can only talk to our Heavenly Father via prayer.

Therefore beloved, in every situation, pray. Are you persecuted, pray.

Are you always misunderstood, pray

Are you sick in your body, pray

Are you in debt, work harder and pray

Is your life in danger, pray

Is your foundation broken, pray

Do you always have bad dreams, pray

Is the enemy after your happiness and joy, pray

Have you noticed that they are several adversaries of your open doors, pray

Are there enemies after your destiny, pray

Beloved pray, pray, pray, that is the only weapon. Charms will fail but prayer can never fail. Those you trust to help solve your problems can disappoint you but you will never be disappointed if you go to God in prayer.

Beloved for anything at all, take it to the Lord in prayer for prayer is the answer to it all. Even if you do not have a problem, pray still so you do not fall into temptations or problems.

Jesus understood the importance of not only to pray but to persist and continue to pray until answer comes that was why He told the parable of the unjust Judge. A widow sought for justice continually and disturbed the Judge until he granted her heart desire. Jesus Christ also understood the power of prayer that was why when He was in deep despair, He took some of His trusted disciples to a solitary place to pray. I tell you beloved, if you pray in like manner as Jesus, the Lord whom you seek shall appear suddenly and visit you according to His will. It is in kneeling we win.

NUGGET 109 - The Will Of God For You

Bible Reading: **3 John 1:2**
Beloved, I wish above all things that thou mayest prosper and be in health, even as thy soul prospereth.

Beloved, the will of God for you is to prosper. His will for you is to have good health so you enjoy the prosperity that He has given you. His will is for you to serve Him. His will is for you is to have life and not only to have life but to have it in abundance which means long life. Beloved having known that His will for you is good, how can you activate this will.

It is very simple to activate and actualise the will of God for you. All you have to do is to believe in the word of God and apply it to that situation that is not the will of God for you. The will of the enemy negates the will of God. The word of God says that the enemy's will is always to afflict and to destroy but the will of God is health, prosperity and deliverance. Since the word of God has said the opposite of what the enemy's will has said, believe it and confess it and never stop believing because the enemy will do his best to make you disbelieve, he will increase his afflictions but when you stand firm on what you believe, you will start to conquer and finally defeat him and God's will prevails.

So beloved, whenever the enemy comes to you with what is not God's will for you, remember the will of God for you and believe and speak it, it works.

NUGGET 110 - Always Be Joyful

Bible Reading: **1st Thessalonians 5:16**
Rejoice Evermore.

Beloved, happiness is a choice. You can choose to rejoice evermore just like the word of God has said in 1st Thessalonians 5:16. It means rejoice always no matter the situation. It is possible to find happiness wherever you are in life. The word of God said in everything give thanks and once you cultivate that habit of giving thanks in all situations, joy will not be far from you. This is a powerful habit that will bless you throughout your life. You can run away from relationships, environments, jobs, or even cities just to escape unhappiness but that would never bring solutions to the situations.

Beloved, instead of unhappiness, sorrows, pains and depression that comes with present day situations, embrace joy and happiness. Happiness will keep you strong, resilient, healthy, content and satisfied. Do not forget to recognize the fact that God is watching over you and He is always ready to fill your heart with joy.

CHAPTER 12

Nugget 111
Change Of Clothes

Nugget 112
The Devil Is A Liar

Nugget 113
If He Created The Waster, He Can Destroy The Waster

Nugget 114
But God Meant It Unto Good

Nugget 115
Quench Not The Spirit Bible

Nugget 116
Think On These Things

Nugget 117
If I May But Touch His Garment...

Nugget 118
You Are Who God Says You Are

Nugget 119
Have God's Kind Of Love

Nugget 120
Seek The Lord And He Shall Notice You

NUGGET 111 - Change Of Clothes

Bible Reading: **Zechariah 3:3 -4**
Now Joshua was clothed with filthy garments, and stood before the Angel. And he answered and said unto them that stood before him saying, take away the filthy garments from him. And unto him he said, behold I have caused thy iniquity to pass from thee and I will clothe thee with change of raiment.

Now Joshua was clothed with filthy garments, and stood before the Angel. And he answered and said unto them that stood before him saying, take away the filthy garments from him. And unto him he said, behold I have caused thy iniquity to pass from thee and I will clothe thee with change of raiment.

Joshua was filthy as he stood before the angel of the Lord. This means that Joshua was unclean before the Angel. He went before the presence of the Lord with sin the angel of the Lord instructed the filthy clothes of sin be taken off Joshua and he cleansed him and gave him new clothes to wear.

Beloved, what happened between Joshua and the Angel of the Lord simply shows that we cannot go to the presence of God either to worship, to ask, to give thanks or to praise with filthy heart of unrighteousness or sin. His eyes cannot behold iniquity and so once we appear before the Lord with sin, He turns away and therefore cannot hear us or accept our worship.

There is nothing we can do that will cleanse us but to ask for forgiveness for He is faithful and just to forgive and to cleanse, He will cleanse us with the blood of His son, Jesus. When He cleanses us, we gain new clothes just like Joshua did and the new clothes is the righteousness of God which enables Him to accept and hear us. So beloved go to Him in like manner and He will answer you.

NUGGET 112 - The Devil Is A Liar

Bible Reading: John 8:44
Ye are of your father the devil, and the lusts of your father ye will do. He was a murderer from the beginning, and abode not in the truth, because there's no truth in him. When he speaketh a lie, he speaketh of his own: for he is a liar and the father of it.

Ye are of your father the devil, and the lusts of your father ye will do. He was a murderer from the beginning, and abode not in the truth, because there's no truth in him. When he speaketh a lie, he speaketh of his own: for he is a liar and the father of it.

The scriptures established the fact that the devil is a liar and the father of all lies. He has no iota of truth in him, he lives in lies and has been lying from the very beginning. Beloved if this description of the devil by the word of God and from Christ Himself is true then why do we as believers believe the devil most times when he speaks into our ears.

The devil is good at whispering to our ears such things as "you can't make it" those good jobs are not for people like you" "you can't be healed" you can't make heaven, you can't live a holy life " can't you see that God has forgotten you" "you can't make it in life" you can't build that house with this your little earnings" you are a failure" "all your mates are making it, they are all better than you". Beloved, all those whispers from the devil are all lies, he has never said the truth and can never start saying the truth now especially to you, a child of God. He hates you and always wants you to sin against God by doubting Him. The devil told Eve in Gen. 3:4 "you shall not surely die" when God had already told her and Adam in Gen. 2:17 that the day they eat of the tree of knowledge of good and evil, they shall surely die. The word of God said that the devil is subtle and deceitful. Do not listen to him, rather believe what the word of God has said because unlike the devil, God can never lie. A song writer said "whose report will you believe?". Beloved believe the report of God concerning you and not what that devil is saying because he is a liar and the father of all lies.

NUGGET 113 - If He Created The Waster, He Can Destroy The Waster

Bible Reading: Isaiah 54:16
Behold I have created the Smith that bloweth the coals in the fire and that bringeth forth an instrument for his work; and I have created the Waster to destroy.

A waster is one who destroys. The waster targets good things. Herod was a waster as well as Pharoah. Troublers and enemies of our destinies are equally wasters. Beloved, do you know that most times the so called enemies of your destinies are actually raised by God just for Him to be glorified. At times, God creates difficult times so He can prove Himself as 'The Almighty', the one who has the absolute power to deliver and to save.

He created the wasters, He knows the components with which He created the wasters and therefore knows how to dismantle the wasters as well. Beloved with this fact at the back of your mind, know that the troubles you are passing through now might be God trying to prove Himself as the all powerful God to you. It might be that He wants to use that situation to make you stronger and better. It might be that He has raised that waster to take you to your divine destiny.

Also know that wasters created by God Himself cannot kill nor destroy you, somewhere and somehow along the line, God will show up for you because if He Has the ability to create the waster, He also has the ability to destroy the waster.

NUGGET 114 - But God Meant It Unto Good

Bible Reading: **Genesis 50:20**
As for you; ye thought evil against me; but God meant it unto good, to bring to pass, as it is this day, to save much people alive.

As for you; ye thought evil against me; but God meant it unto good, to bring to pass, as it is this day, to save much people alive.

Beloved some unfavourable situations most times are blessings in disguise. The scripture said that we should count it all joy when we fall into diverse trials for they work out good in the long run. The scripture also said that all things work out together for good to those who love God. The condition here is to love and fear God. The evil Joseph's brethren plotted for him would not have turned out for good for him if he had no the fear of God in him.

The emphasis here is to love God with all your heart and serve Him with fear and reverence. So beloved, it is important we maintain our stand in the Lord when we are going through situations if not, those situations might overcome and defeat us and we might not be able to declare like Joseph to our enemies who wish us evil that "you thought evil against me; but God meant it unto good." Let us therefore love and fear God so that He would fight our battles and turn all evil by our enemies to good.

NUGGET 115 - Quench Not The Spirit

Bible Reading: 1st Thessalonians 5:19
Quench not the Spirit.

Beloved, if we obey the Holy Spirit we can never go wrong. The Holy Spirit is our partner, He is our Director. Just like the end product of a movie would not be perfect and well finished if the characters did not listen to or carry out the directions and instructions of the Director, so also our lives and actions will not be perfect without strict adherence to the directions of the Holy Spirit. He is the Driver that helps us get to our eternal destinations which is heaven. Just like a vehicle without a driver cannot move, function or get to its destination so can we not without the Holy Spirit function or move according to the will of God to please and to obey Him.

The Holy Spirit is a personality. He usually accompanies us all the time if we let Him. He is usually that small still voice that rebukes us instantly when we go wrong or commit sin against God. Most times we often ignore that small still voice or try to suppress and shut Him down but we often later realise that listening and obeying Him would have been a better option. This is because any disobedience to the Holy Spirit usually has grave consequences.

Beloved, if we want to live right, if we want to make heaven, if we want good directions of any kind, if we want life and our Christian lives and journeys to be easier, we should always listen to the voice of the Holy Spirit. If we do, we will never go wrong.

NUGGET 116 - Think On These Things

Bible Reading: **Philippians 4:8**
Finally, my brethren, whatsoever that are true, whatsoever things are honest, whatsoever things that are just, whatsoever things that are pure, whatsoever things that are lovely, whatsoever things are of good report; if there be any virtue, if there be any praise, think on these things.

Finally, my brethren, whatsoever that are true, whatsoever things are honest, whatsoever things that are just, whatsoever things that are pure, whatsoever things that are lovely, whatsoever things are of good report; if there be any virtue, if there be any praise, think on these things.

In Philippians 4:8, Apostle Paul listed the things upon which Christians must meditate on and all of them are positive things. He encouraged believers to bring their minds and imaginations under control; to keep their minds on what is pure, true, noble, lovely and admirable.

Beloved, are you seeking to live the life God wants you to live, are you seeking to have life and have it more abundantly, think positively. Focus on that which is right, true, lovely and pure. Concentrate on those things Apostle Paul listed and that would make you optimistic about life. There is no room in the christian mentality for pessimistic thinking only positive thinking. Have the mindset that all things are under the control of the God who can do all things and you will see the best things of life.

Let your focus and thoughts be on that which is good and after the nature of God who is working together all things for good for you and your life will be filled with good things.

NUGGET 117 - If I May But Touch His Garment...

Bible Reading: Mathew 9:21
And she said within herself if I may but touch His garment, I shall be whole.

The woman with a blood disease for decades and according to the scriptures, had spent all her money on doctors, and I am sure she had tried the herbalist too and many prayer houses but her situation was no better.

We shall learn few things from this woman. Please note that this woman after trying several means and did not any get better, decided to try Jesus because she must have heard about Him and how He went about healing the sick and the oppressed. She got tired of going to places without solutions. She did not know that instead of going to physicians, she would have gone to Jesus and the problem would not have lingered for 12 years. This shows that some steps could take you immediately to your miracle or far away from your miracle.

Secondly the woman thought in her heart "If I may but touch his garment." Her thought simply demonstrates faith. Her faith took virtue out of Jesus and remember Jesus can never take faith for granted. He grants your request once He sees your faith. Beloved, whoever that comes to Jesus must first of all believe. You have to have faith that once you tell it to Jesus, the matter is solved. The result of your faith is that your miracle will no longer linger.

Everyone was touching Jesus but that woman's touch was exceptional because she touched with faith.

Beloved have you considered telling Jesus about those issues you have been handling all alone for all these years. Do not keep mute and think that God sees your heart and knows you need solutions. You have to go to Him just like the woman did. You have to seek Him, you have to talk to Jesus for a problem shared with only human is half solved not to talk of a problem shared with Jesus, the greatest problem solver and you will receive instance answers.

NUGGET 118 - You Are Who God Says You Are

Bible Reading: Mathew 16:15 -16
But He saith unto them, but whom say ye that I am? And Simon Peter answered and said, thou art the Christ, the Son of the living God.

Beloved, you are what God says you are, not what anyone says you are, not what any of your present situations says you are, not what the country nor the society in which you find yourself says you are.

Jesus asked His disciples who men say He is and Peter answered that He is the Christ, the son of the living God of which Jesus declared that flesh and blood could not have revealed such an answer to Peter but God himself.

Jesus declaration only means that it is only God that can reveal who we really are not anyone else not even the so called oracles people consult these days. It also means that circumstances cannot reveal we are or define us.

Once we know who we are which God had revealed to us through His words and Christ Jesus, we do not accept any other identity even if the devil is trying so hard to put it to us. We are to refuse vehemently, the identity the devil and circumstances are trying to define us with and stick to the identity God had already given us in Christ Jesus. We should work with that God's identity and live it to full manifestation and perfection.

Jesus heard all His disciples' responses on the question He asked about His identity and immediately affirmed Peter's response because He knows himself. He also knows that only His Heavenly Father knows whom He really is and had revealed it to Peter and not any man.

So beloved, do not let the devil give you a name God has not given you. Do not agree with devil to describe you by the negative situations he brings your way. Do not let anyone describe you with a name God that knows you very well has not given you. By so doing, you will remain who God says you are.

If God says you are a winner, do not let the devil give you the name looser, if God says you are rich in health, wealth, faith, righteousness of God and every other good name which the mouth of the Lord has named you, do not ever answer a contrary name no matter how much pressure the devil exerts on you to do so.

Beloved, God and His words said that you are a chosen race, a dearly beloved of Him, free from condemnations through Christ and that you are healed through His stripes. God said that you can do all things through Christ, He said you are washed by the blood of Jesus Christ and that you are the salt of the earth. God said you are the light of the world, completely forgiven, rich through the poverty of Christ and that you are alive and will not die because He died. All these and many more are what God said you are so do not let the devil or anyone he uses tell you otherwise.

NUGGET 119 - Have God's Kind Of Love

Bible Reading: **John 3:16**
For God so loved the world that He gave His only begotten son, that whosoever believeth in Him should not perish but have everlasting life.

God's love for the world prompted Him to give His most treasured treasure, His son, Jesus Christ. How can you demonstrate the love of God? How can you demonstrate the love for your society? What have you given back to the society that you love just like God Himself loved the word and gave.

What about the love we have for one another, how have you been able to prove that love?. Just like God proved His by giving His son, have you given what your brother is in need of? It may not necessarily be financial need, what about word of encouragement or prayer or even giving the gospel of our Lord Jesus Christ to an unbelieving brother for the salvation of his soul.

Beloved, let us love and demonstrate God's kind of love even in the littlest ways.

NUGGET 120 - Seek The Lord And He Shall Notice You

Bible Reading: **Luke 19:3 -5**
And he sought to see Jesus who He was and could not for the press because he was a little of stature.
4. And he ran before and climbed unto sycamore tree to see him, for He was to pass that way.
☐.And when Jesus came to the place He looked up and saw him and said unto him, Zacchaeus make haste and come down, for today, I must abide at thy house.

Beloved, it is good to seek the Lord, the scripture recorded that Zacchaeus sought to see Jesus but he had inhibitions. The crowd and his stature prevented him from seeing Jesus but even at those inhibitors he earnestly wanted to see Jesus and he devised a means by climbing the tree.

The scriptures recorded that when Jesus saw the eagerness and sincerity of heart of Zacchaeus to see Him, He took notice of him and singled him out from the whole crowd. As a result of his action, He(Jesus) visited and dined with him and it is a very great honour and privilege to be visited by the Savior himself. Zacchaeus' life never remained the same again after that visit by Jesus. This shows that if we seek Jesus with all our hearts and in all sincerity and if we make tangible or little eff ort to see Jesus despite all obstacles and pains of life, He will definitely appear to us. He loves us to seek Him, He wants us to establish some strong ties and close relationship with Him.

So beloved, seek to know more about Jesus and He will notice you and come to you and your life will never be the same again. Your life will definitely change for the better.

CHAPTER 13

Nugget 121
Are You A Special Seed?

Nugget 122
We Are More Than Conquerors

Nugget 123
He Took Our Place

Nugget 124
The Love Of Money Is The Root Of All Evil

Nugget 125
Seek God On Time Bible

Nugget 126
Be Vigilant!

Nugget 127
Be A Friend Of God

Nugget 128
But If It Dies, It Bringeth Forth Much Fruits

Nugget 129
God Respects And Honours His Word

Nugget 130
Train Up A Child

NUGGET 121 - Are You A Special Seed?

Bible Reading: 1st Peter 2:9
But ye are a chosen generation, a royal priesthood, an holy nation, a peculiar people; that ye should shew forth the praises of Him who hath called you out of darkness into His marvellous light.

Beloved, it is important we note that some seeds are special and that God takes particular interest in them. God's torch light is constantly on them; they cannot afford to do certain things. What others do and get away with, they cannot because of God's interest and likeness towards them. He is jealous over them so He would not allow them serve other gods but Him. Some would even try to run away from Him like Jonah did but He would not let them. He still pursues them and most times lands them with people or places or things that would never allow them run too far from Him. Jonah was that kind of seed.

God's interest was on Jonah, he tried to run away from God but God caught up with him; God commanded a fish to keep him from running farther away from Him. He protected him in the belly of the fish. He even supplied him with oxygen in the belly of the fish and did not allow him die of hunger or dehydration. Beloved, that is how far God can go if you are a special seed and He is interested in you. The most interesting part is that no matter where the seed of God's interest runs to or how far they run, He still catches up with them and uses them to His own glory.

God later used Jonah for the purpose for which He wanted.

On Jonah's part, he later surrendered to God and allowed God to use him do what He wanted, he carried out that special assignment after all.

Beloved, have you noticed that God's special interest is in you? Are the situations around you pointing to the fact that God wants you? Do you constantly have the feeling that God has called you out to be a special seed unto Him and to serve Him? Have you been told and it has been confirmed that you are a special seed unto God? Please do not hesitate anymore, yield yourself to Him, allow that seed of greatness in you to manifest. If you are a chosen seed according to the scriptures then show forth the praises of Him who had singled you out and called you.

NUGGET 122 - We Are More Than Conquerors

Bible Reading: **Romans 8:37**
Nay, in all these things, we are more than conquerors through Him that loved us.

Beloved, all things work together for good to them that love and fear God. Battles, afflictions, sicknesses, temptations, trials are inevitable on our Christian journeys. In fact, they are all tools to our victory for how can you say you are victorious without fighting any battle, how can you have a testimony without trials, how can you say you passed a test without an examination, how can you experience the healing power of Jesus without first falling sick. You cannot confidently say you are a winner in the Lord Jesus without you engaging in some contests. You cannot obtain a crown of life without having endured temptations and trials.

The moment you believed and accepted the Lord Jesus Christ as your Lord and Saviour, the moment you rejected the devil and his ways and the moment you started loving Jesus and doing His words and works, a battle, a war, a conflict began. Unfortunately, that war never ends until you get to heaven. You will find out that when you finish one battle another one emerges, the battle even becomes fiercer as you advance in your journey with Christ but the good news is that in all these battles you are more than conqueror through Christ who loves us and with Him by your side the devil can never ever win the battle for even when it seems you are loosing the battle Jesus will always step in at the right time to help.

Beloved, your own is to be strong in the Lord and in the power of His might and put on the whole necessary armour of Christ that you might be able to win this war. (Ephesians 6:10-18).

NUGGET 123 - He Took Our Place

Bible Reading: **Isaiah 53:5**
But He was wounded for our transgressions, he was bruised for our iniquities: the chastisement of our peace was upon Him; and with His stripes we are healed.

Beloved this is coming to you to remind you that He took your place. Have you ever watched a movie or seen in reality when someone took a bullet that was meant for a loved one so that loved one could live? It means the person who took the bullet in place of the other died so the other could live; that is exactly what Christ did for you and I on the cross. Christ became a sinner so you can be righteous. He died the most shameful and worst death so that you might live and that you might have eternal life. He was condemned so that you and I will not be condemned.

In Isaiah 53:5, the scripture says He was wounded for our transgressions; He was bruised for our iniquities and the chastisement of our peace was upon Him and by His stripes we are healed. This simply means that everything that happened to Him on the way to the cross and on the cross was just for us. It means that the wounds and the bruises were for our transgressions and iniquities, the chastisement and the stripes were for our peace and for our healing.

Beloved, what is it that is troubling you and what is it that you need and what is that the devil is planning for you and what lies is he telling you? Just know that everything was settled for you on the cross by the reason of the death of Jesus Christ. He took your place when He died on the cross. An exchange of death for life was made immediately He gave up the Ghost and when He said on the cross that "it is finished", it means that all your troubles, sorrows, pains, disappointments, failures, sicknesses and diseases are all finished and taken care of. So go with the consciousness and belief that He took your place and has taken all your troubles of life and sins away and you will smile the rest of your life.

NUGGET 124 - The Love Of Money Is The Root Of All Evil

Bible Reading: **1st Timothy 2:10**
For the love of money is the root of all evil: which while some coveted after, they have erred from the faith and pierced themselves through with many sorrows.

Beloved, we know that money is good and we also know that money answereth all things and without money most essential needs of life may not be met. Yes, we need money so that the gospel will spread etc but according to the scriptures, it is not money that is evil. What is evil is the materialistic heart that is obsessed with obtaining it; the love for money.

The Bible takes such a strong position against loving money because of the power we give to money and the evils born out of the love for money. Some people place a greater emphasis on gaining and gaining money and like the brethren in Ephesus, they stray from the faith because of desire and quest to be rich. And in their desire to satisfy their thirst for money they marginalised their relationship with friends, family, other Christians and even God and a little compromise here and a little compromise there, evils begin to breed accompanied with sorrows. Beloved, it ought not to be so, we should never allow the desire to make money overwhelm us to the extent that we forget our Christian values and principles and our faith.

NUGGET 125 - Seek God On Time

Bible Reading: **Isaiah 55:6**
Seek ye the Lord while He may be found; call ye upon Him while He is near.

Isaiah 55:6 instructed us to seek God on time and when He is near. This does not mean that God is not always around us or that He is late but there is always the right time to get His attention and there is actually a time you might seek God and He will not be found. A sinner who received several warnings from God and His messengers to repent from his sins when he had the time to, will seek God and will not find Him if he finds himself in hellfire. So the sinner's best choice is to seek God now that He can be found.

Moment of worship brings down God's presence nearer to us and that' is why it is always wise to worship God first to bring His presence down to us before asking Him for anything. Beloved, seize that moment of worship to ask God for anything. Have you also noticed that prayers made at midnight hours are always eff ective? Seize that moment too.

Beloved, it is strongly advised that once you have a bad dream; do not wait until you start seeing the signs of the dream coming to pass before you start praying. Call on God on time by immediately praying against the dream and He will avert it rather than waiting until the damage is done. The same goes to all other things, ask on time, do not let God be the last option or the last person you will resort to.

NUGGET 126 - Be Vigilant!

Bible Reading: **1st Peter 5:8**
Be sober, be vigilant; because your adversary the devil, as a roaring lion, walking about, seeking whom he may devour.

Beloved, these are the last days. The enemy, the devil and the powers of darkness he works with are all out and about seeking whom to devour, whom to deviate from the faith and seeking whom to destroy. There is a red alert that the kingdom of darkness are all out for massive recruitment to their kingdom being that their time is little and they need to meet their target before the end of age.

Apostle Peter, in 1st Peter 5:8 said that Satan roams about as a nervous and hungry lion. His preys are usually the children of God and not those already in his camp. The devil and those working for him have lounged a massive attack on the children of God. Beloved, I hope you know that you cannot see the devil physically; he works through his agents and he can also work through manipulating your mind to believe lies against God and His kingdom. He also uses friends and his followers to talk you into lies and mirages that do not actually exit when you truly analyse them but note that the devil cannot voluntarily devour you except you let him. It is therefore necessary we the children of God learn how the devil seeks to destroy the lives of men and how he stalks his prey, keeping track of them right from the womb until he is able to strike.

Also remember that the devil knows you very well and he knows what you like most and those are the things he will use to entice you to him. Apostle Peter hence warns that we be alert! We be cautious! We be careful! We be vigilant! We be mature Christians less we fall victim to his hunger for souls of men and loose our faith and our salvation then, heaven.

Beloved, it is very important you always be in the spirit and avoid sin so that God will always show you when they are about to strike and where they are coming from and what to do. Never leave His presence or allow His presence to leave you. Always strive to please Him and most importantly maintain a good and close relationship with Him. If you draw near to Him, He will draw near to you. If you are close to God, He will always make all the devil's plans known to you ahead of time and you will definitely defeat him.

NUGGET 127 - Be A Friend Of God

Bible Reading: James 2:23
And the scripture was fulfilled which saith; Abraham believed God, and it was imputed unto him for righteousness: and he was called the friend of God.

Who is a friend? A friend is someone you can confide in. A person you know very well and regard with affection and trust. Beloved are you a friend of God? Can God be able to boast about you to the devil just like He did with Job? Can you equally boast that you know God very well as much as you said you do? Can God trust you to represent Him well on this earth? Can you also trust God to have your back always and not fear anything? Can you trust God to keep you and not fall at the slightest test or temptation? Do you love God with all your heart and mind?

It is very simple to become a friend of God. Just emulate Abraham, a friend of God. What qualified him to be a friend of God? The scripture said he feared God, he obeyed God, he taught his family to know God; he communed with God all the time, he believed God and it was imputed him for righteousness and he was called a friend of God.

Beloved, the best friend to have is God. Friends may fail but He never fails, you can tell Him just anything; you can converse with Him the way you converse with human. God is a friend that sticks closer than a brother. Do you have a complaint to make? Go to Him and lay the complaint He is more attentive, more objective and He will give the best advice and the best direction ever. Do you have a problem that needs to be solved? Go to your friend, God, He will give the best solution, that is one of the numerous benefits of being a friend of God.

NUGGET 128 - But If It Dies, It Bringeth Forth Much Fruits

Bible Reading: **John 12:24**
Verily, verily, I say unto you except a corn of wheat fall into the ground and die, it abideth alone: but if it die, it bringeth forth much fruits.

Beloved we are seeds of God and as seeds we are to reproduce our kinds. John 12:24 explained that except a seed falls to the ground and dies it abides alone but if it dies, it produces many seeds of its kind. This spiritually means that Christ died so He can save us. He died so that every of God's seed can inherit His kingdom. If He died so He can save us; what about us? Are we saving others too just like we were saved? We as seeds are to reproduce our kinds. We are saved to save others.

One of the ways to save others is through evangelism. In Mark 16:15, Jesus made it clear to the fact that He wants us to preach the gospel to everyone. He wants us to save others just like He saved us by teaching them to know Him. Beloved, how many people have you spoken to about Christ? how many souls have you brought to Christ since you got saved? You can start from your Jerusalem, that is your household. Start with that your Uncle or that your Aunty or Cousin that is yet to know Christ. You can speak to them about Christ while discussing family matters with them. You can go out and share leaflets about the gospel and pray the Holy Spirit to interpret to them and bring them to know Christ. You can also talk to that person you are working with that needs to hear about Christ. You can even pray for anyone you know that needs Christ to come to repentance and know Christ.

Let us not allow the devil take over the world because nowadays the devil's disciples are preaching openly for people to accept him. Beloved, whichever way you choose, let us make Christ known to all men. Let us reproduce our kinds.

NUGGET 129 - God Respects And Honours His Word

Bible Reading: Ps 138:2
I will worship toward thy holy temple, and praise thy name for thy loving kindness and for thy truth: for thou hast magnified thy word above all thy name.

God respects His word more than His name; reminding God of His words when asking Him for anything makes it mandatory for Him to give you what you asked for because it will make Him a liar if He does not and God can never lie.

Beloved, whatever you are looking for is in the word of God. If you are looking for power, the word of God said in Luke 10:19 behold I give unto you power. Are you looking for promotion? It is in His word, Ps 75:6-7 promotion cometh not from anywhere but from God. Are you looking for healing for your body? Isaiah 53:5 said with His stripes we are healed. Are you looking for money? His word said in Deut 8:18, He is the one that gives us power to make wealth. Are you looking for protection? In Ps 91:11, He said He will give His angels charge over you. Are you looking for favour? It is also in His word-Ps 5:12, with favour He will compass you as with a shield. What about longevity? He said in Ps 91:16, with long life He will satisfy you. Are you looking for Success, deliverance, salvation etc? They are all in the word of God.

Therefore, beloved, the need for you to study and know the word of God cannot be over emphasized. You need the word of God, it is applicable in all facets of life not only to meet your physical needs but your spiritual needs as well. The word nourishes your soul and keeps it healthy and ready for eternity with Christ in heaven. The word keeps you away from sin (your word have I hid in my heart that I may not sin against you). The word of God gives life to your body and to your soul.

Endeavor to find time out of your tight schedule to study the word of God and get yourself acquainted with it and you will find life easier.

NUGGET 130 - Train Up A Child

Bible Reading: **Proverb 22:6**
Train up a child in the way he should go: and when he is old, he will not depart from it.

Children are leaders of tomorrow, they are future Christians. They will be the ones to replace all the giant men and women of God of today when they are gone. Imagine if we do not train them or raise them to be godly children and good ambassadors for Christ, who is going to be Christians when we are gone, who is going to represent Christ in the future. None of us will live forever, we need people, giants in the Lord who will take over the baton from us.

Beloved, there is therefore need to raise our children according to the Lord's ways. The scripture above said that they will not depart from those ways when they grow older. God wants us as parents to live lives of integrity as examples for our children. livelivesofintegrityasexamplesforourchildren. God said in Genesis 18:19 that He knew that Abraham will direct his sons and their families to keep His ways by doing what is right and just.

Beloved, do not be too busy and neglect your children's spiritual needs, as you are meeting their physical needs also remember their spiritual needs as well. You need to make out time for them out of your busy schedule to teach them the rich Bible stories and biblical principles to help them learn the right ways to treat others and also inculcate in them long lasting values that will help them form good characters and behaviors.

Remember whatever they will be tomorrow starts from now. Also remember that you would be needing them tomorrow when you grow old and feeble. How can they be there for you if you neglect to train them to be good Christians and show them the right ways. Remember too that we all will give account of every child that the Lord gave to us on the last day.

CHAPTER 14

Nugget 131
You Are The Children Of The Most High

Nugget 132
God's Love Will Never Wane Nor Die

Nugget 133
Whosever Is Born Of God Does Not Commit Sin

Nugget 134
The Blood Of Jesus Speaks

Nugget 135
He Shall Have Whatever He Saith.

Nugget 136
You Are Seed

Nugget 137
Do Not Forsake The Assembly Of One Another

Nugget 138
The Eyes Of The Lord Is On Those Who Are Wrongly Hated

Nugget 139
Be Alone With God In Prayer

Nugget 140
God Is Our Daddy, Tell It To Him

NUGGET 131 - You Are The Children Of The Most High

Bible Reading: Psalms 82:6
I have said, ye are gods and all of you are the children of the Most High.

Beloved, we are the children of our father God by our belief in the Lord Jesus Christ His son. The moment we believe, we are translated from the kingdom of darkness into the kingdom of God and we drop our old nature and assume the nature of God just like a child born into a particular family takes that family's genes and nature by virtue of birth.

If we now have the nature of God and He has the power to create, we too have the same power. We can create whatever we want with the words of our mouth because there is power in spoken words. God calleth those things that are not as if they were; we too can do same and that is called faith. Call forth whatever you need and believe it is there already.

God is powerful, we too can be powerful by constant communion with Him, dwelling in His secret place, seeking His face and studying His word.

God is love, we can be love too by loving others

God is merciful and compassionate; we can be that too by having tender heart towards people, being sensitive to people's needs and showing empathy.

God hates sin; we too should hate and abhor sin.

God is forgiving, we should be forgiving too

God is kind; we too should be kind towards one another.

Beloved, be and act like your father, God. Remember an apple does not fall very far from its tree and a Lion gives birth to a Lion.

NUGGET 132 - God's Love Will Never Wane Nor Die

Bible Reading: Lamentations 3:22&23
It is of the Lord's mercies that we are not consumed, because His compassions fail not.
They are new every morning: great is thy faithfulness.

Beloved, God's love for us His children is endless, it never decreases, it never fades, it is renewed day in and day out. Oh what a love! The scripture says that as each day breaks, God renews His mercy towards us because He loves us; He allows us to enjoy His grace, goodness, forgiveness, faithfulness and compassion even in our low and sinful state.

One of the interesting part is that He is pitiful, He sees our troubles and out of pity reaches out to rescue us. Another interesting part of God's love is its unchanging nature. God can never say "I do not love you anymore" to any of His. His love does not expire; the scripture says that even if we sin against Him, He will chastise us with the rod of men but His love and faithfulness will never be taken away from us.

Beloved, think of the love you have for your children, how you feel towards them and how you feel when they are in need of good things; that love is nothing compares to God's love for us. A song writer says it is so high, so deep and so strong.

Therefore Beloved, go ahead and enjoy God's love and remember never to forget to reciprocate such love by never going away from Him so that His love will be yours to enjoy forever.

NUGGET 133 - Whosever Is Born Of God Does Not Commit Sin

Bible Reading: 1st John 3:9
Whosoever is born of God doth not commit sin; for His seed remaineth in him: and he cannot sin, because he is born of God.

According to the word of God, we are seed of God by our belief in God and His son Christ Jesus whom through His blood made us sons and daughters of God. As seed, we are characterized as dead to sin.

Seed dies spiritually to sin. If we are truly born of Him then according to 1st John 3:9, we cannot continue to sin because we are His seed and therefore we are carrying His nature.

Beloved since we are seed, we no longer allow sin to control us or reign in our mortal bodies; the moment we accept and put on Christ, we become dead to sin and alive in Christ having dominion over sin. Though we find it difficult most times and struggle with sin, the spirit of God in us helps and empowers us to overcome and be no longer enslaved to sin.

Apostle Paul in Romans 12:1&2 encouraged us as seed to dedicate our bodies to the Lord and live a life of holiness to please Him; he also encouraged us as seed not to live the kind of life that the world lives. This means that as seed, we no longer live the way we used to live, we no longer follow after the pattern of the world; we now live a totally different kind of life.

Beloved, therefore, to be qualified to be called seed of God and to partake of the promises thereof, we must be born again. We must put on Christ, we must live a holy life pleasing and acceptable unto God our father and there must be a notable difference between the life we used to live and the life we live now. We cannot do it on our own, we have the Holy Spirit to help us live that life that God approved.

NUGGET 134 - The Blood Of Jesus Speaks

Bible Reading: Hebrews 12:24
And to Jesus the mediator of a new covenant, and to the blood of sprinkling, that speaketh better things than that of Abel.

Beloved, do you know that the blood of Jesus speaks? Yes! It does. What does it speak? Better things!! What is the enemy and the devil speaking against you at the moment? What is the situation of the country speaking today? What are the rulers of darkness, principalities and powers speaking against you today? What is the powers of your father's house and that of your mother's house speaking against you now? What have the doctors said concerning you at your recent or previous visit to the hospital? What are the symptoms in your body saying? What is your present immigration status saying? What is your bank account at the moment saying? What is the present condition of your home saying and what is your marital status saying at the moment? Beloved whatever it is that is saying anything; the BLOOD OF JESUS is speaking better things than them all.

The blood of Jesus has tremendous powers and it does not loose its potency and it does not loose its flow. The blood of Jesus speaks and will continue to speak and it speaks forever. The blood is made available to all who believe and it is a weapon of the believers against the devil. So use the blood of Jesus today and let it speak for you better things than the devil is speaking or have spoken against you and all aspects of you. Whenever the devil is speaking against, the blood of Jesus speaks for.

NUGGET 135 - "...He Shall Have Whatever He Saith."

Bible Reading: **Mark 11:23**
For verily I say unto you, that whosoever shall say unto this mountain, be thou removed and be thou cast into the sea; and shall not doubt in his heart, but shall believe that those things which he saith shall come to pass; he shall have whatever he saith.

Beloved, let us study Mark 11:23 the is and draw some lessons out of it. Jesus cursed the unfruitful fig tree to wither by simple mere words of command and the disciples found out later that the fig tree actually withered at His words. He afterwards told them that they can do same if they have faith in God. It is worthy to note that Jesus said 'whosoever' and this simply means that everyone including you and I can move mountains.

Mark 11:23 did not say that only Pastors or Prophets or Bishops can move mountains but anyone who believes. Most times when we are faced with problems (mountains) we wait for Pastors and Prophets to pray for us for solutions or to remove the mountains. Some people even go as far as paying money for prayers to be made for them. Beloved, whosoever includes you, you can handle it, learn to do it yourself for you have all it takes, you only need to have Jesus as your lord and saviour and have faith in God. Once you have Jesus and you are true to Him by serving Him in truth and in spirit, you have free access to God anytime and any day. You have as much right as your Pastor, Bishop and the Reverend to pray to God and He will answer.

NUGGET 136 - You Are Seed

Bible Reading: Galatians 3:29
And if ye be Christ's, then are ye Abraham's seed, and heirs according to the promise.

A seed in this context is an off spring; a descendant. God made a promise to bless Abraham and his seed immeasurably. In Galatians 3:16, the scripture made emphasis of the singular use of the word seed not plural-seeds, which means that that seed of Abraham referred to here is one singular seed which is Christ, our saviour.

Furthermore, Galatians 3:29 tells us that if we are Christ's then we are that Abraham seed and heirs to the promise. 1st Corinthians 6:17 tells us that he who is joined with Christ is one with Him and Galatians 3:27 tells us that we have put on Christ and this simply means that we are Christ and Christ is us; we are in Him and He is in us and that we are seed of Abraham by faith through Christ, our saviour.

Beloved if we are Christ's and therefore Abraham's seed, we have every access to those promises God made to Abraham found in Genesis 12&17 which are that the Lord will multiply us exceedingly, make us fathers of all nations, make us exceedingly fruitful, the Lord will make Kings come out of our lineages, He will be a God unto us and unto our generations. The Lord will give us lands in which we are strangers to possess for ever, He will bless us, He will make our names great, He will make us blessings to others and bless those that bless us. The Lord will curse those that curse us and through us, all our families will be blessed.

Beloved, claim these promises every day for they are all yours, even if you cannot see them manifesting, do not give up, continue to claim them; they will surely manifest.

NUGGET 137 - Do Not Forsake The Assembly Of One Another

Bible Reading: **Hebrews 10:25**
Not forsaking the assembling of ourselves together, as the manner of some is; but exhorting one another: and so much the more, as ye see the days approaching.

Beloved, going to the house of God to worship Him and to fellowship with brethren in Christ is paramount for spiritual exhortation. How do you feel when they say let us go to the house of God? Do you feel like the Psalmist in Psalms 122:1? Have you ever been in God's presence and how do you feel when true, pure fire worshippers raise beautiful worship songs to God with fine tuned, well harmonised musical instruments and instrumentalists? Beloved, even without musical instruments, the feeling is awesome; you get lost in His presence; sometimes you even cry because you feel His presence deep within and around you; at that moment your soul is connected to Him in worship and anything is possible from healing to deliverance to salvation etc. What about when God's word comes through His vessel? You get filled up spiritually and equipped, ready to face the world and the devils therein.

Beloved, it is so sweet to be in the presence of the Lord and never forsake the assembly of God's people because of its high spiritual benefits to your soul. Jesus is always there (Mathew 18:20) to meet your physical and spiritual needs. The blood of Jesus is always there to cleanse you from all sins. You get to hear the word of God to guide you in your daily christian life unto godliness, righteousness and holiness that will take you to heaven.

Yes you can worship God anywhere including your house but what about your gifts which are for the edification of one another and the body of Christ. Let others benefit from your gifts and let God be exalted and even if you do not have any, go to the house of God and let the gifts of others impact your life. There is no better place to be than the house of God. In His presence your soul is built up. So, Beloved, make it a custom to always go the house of God just like Jesus did (Luke 4:16) and your soul will have a beautiful experience with God each day.

NUGGET 138 - The Eyes Of The Lord Is On Those Who Are Hated Wrongfully

Bible Reading: **Gen 29:31**
And when the Lord saw that a Leah was hated, He opened her womb, but Racheal was barren.

God's gaze and eyes are fixed specially upon those that are wrongfully hated. A case in point is Leah in Genesis 29:31. The scripture described that the Lord saw that Leah was hated which means that the eye of the Lord is upon the sufferer, the hated and the persecuted and He always compensate them.

Leah was a wife of priority but not of preference and it is remarkable that that same wife of priority and not of preference is the mother of the seed in whom all nations are to be blessed. Therefore, Beloved, be relaxed when you are not loved by those you expected to love you or hated by those you have helped in one way or the other or even when you have people who are wrongfully your enemies. The scripture said that the eye of the Lord is upon you and He knows how best to handle the situation.

NUGGET 139 - Be Alone With God In Prayer

Bible Reading: **Mathew 6:6**
But thou, when thou prayest, enter into thy closet, and when thou hast shut thy door, pray to to thy Father which is in secret; and thy Father which seeth in secret, shall reward thee openly.

Spiritual exercise gives us room to be intimate with your father. Always be alone with your father communicating with Him through prayers. A child who always spends time alone with his father gets to know the father very well and is better with the father than the rest of the children who do not have time to spend with their father alone. A child who usually spends more time with the father alone usually forms a special bond with the father than the rest of the children who do not. The child who spends more time with the father always has some edge over others who do not and that attracts a special blessing, love and favour from the father and can even become his father's favourite child. The father always share secrets with him, makes him a priority and gets things done for him easily than others.

Beloved, being alone with God gives you the opportunity to tell Him anything; it gives you the opportunity to discuss your innermost emotions with Him; you can pour out your heart to Him unreservedly. You can equally receive from Him when you are alone with Him. You can receive pardon for your sins because no one can judge and pardon you better than your Heavenly Father. When you receive your father's pardon, the devil and his agents will not have room or legal ground to condemn and attack you.

Also you can hear from Him when you go to Him alone in prayer. He can tell you things you need to know that you do not know. He can direct you on the right path and on the right decisions. You can receive directly from Him without a third party interference. You can call on Him when in trouble and He will answer you.

Beloved, develop a regular prayer pattern, practice it and maintain it, that way you will grow spiritually.

NUGGET 140 - God Is Our Daddy, Tell It To Him

Bible Reading: **Galatians 4:6**
And because ye are sons; God hath sent forth the Spirit of his son into your hearts; crying, Abba father.

If you make a child cry, you might hear that child say to you "I will tell my daddy" That child is saying so because he knows and have confidence that once he tells his daddy, he will do something about the situation. Also if you chase a little child to smack him, he will either run towards his father or his mother to take cover or for protection from you. That child does so because he knows that once he calls his daddy or mummy and runs to them, they will protect and save him from you.

Beloved, God is our father, our daddy. Once you believe that His son, Jesus Christ died for you on the cross for the remission of your sins and you confess with your mouth that He is your Lord and saviour and you start to live a righteous life then you are qualified to call Him Daddy, father. You now have the exclusive right to call Him anytime, any day, for anything at all and He will answer and take care of the situation.

Also you have to form a bond, a relationship with Him as such that you can tell Him just anything even the littlest things like from daddy I have a little headache, please heal me to daddy I am broke please help give me money by giving me a job. You can even say to Him, daddy my supervisor at work is troubling me and I have done nothing to him please help me. Beloved believe me, your daddy will show up and handle the situation and deliver you right on time.

CHAPTER 15

Nugget 141
God Over Answers Prayers

Nugget 142
God Uses The Scriptures To Prepare And Equip His People

Nugget 143
Pray For Leaders And All Men

Nugget 144
Hide The Word Of God

Nugget 145
After That You Have Suff ered A While

Nugget 146
Give God Your Time

Nugget 147
Thou Shall Condemn

Nugget 148
God Is A Covenant Keeping God

Nugget 149
Why Worry When You Can Pray

Nugget 150
The Father Hath Not Left Me Alone

NUGGET 141 - God Over Answers Prayers

Bible Reading: 1st Sam 2:21
And the Lord visited Hannah so that she conceived, and bare three sons and two daughters. And the child Samuel grew before the Lord.

Hannah was a woman of a sorrowful spirit whose adversary mocked year in and year out because of her circumstances but when God visited her, not only did He answered her prayers He over answered her prayers.

God over answered Hannah because she did not feel sorrowful as a result of her problems and did nothing. The scripture said she prayed and wept sore before the Lord (1st Sam 1:10), she vowed a vow (1st Sam 1:11), she continued praying and did not give up (1st Sam 1:12) and she spoke to the Lord from her heart (1st Sam 1:13) then God visited her.

Beloved, are your adversaries mocking and provoking you to tears all the time? Are they asking you where is your God? Are you so troubled with issues you do not know how to handle and you are already slipping into depression mode? Try and adopt Hannah's methods and see if God will not over answer.

NUGGET 142 - God Uses The Scriptures To Prepare And Equip His People

Bible Reading: **2nd Timothy 3:17**
That the man of God may be perfect. Thoroughly furnished unto good works.

Beloved, have you read your bible today? Remember God is closer to us through His words, when you read the word of God, you feel God talking to you. God uses the Scriptures to prepare and equip his people to do every good. God's children can only be perfect through the word of God.

Whatever you need is in the scriptures; be it spiritual or physical needs all is in the word of God. Anything at all you need be it a boost of physical or spiritual energy or guidance or protection or health and the rest; just open up the word of God and you can find whatever you are looking. Even if you are looking for encouragement and spurring on, the place to go is the word of God. God uses His word to tell you what you need to hear so you can be prepared for whatever you may encounter daily and in your life.

Beloved, rise up and read up if you have not and you will hear the Lord speak to you and prepare you for good works.

NUGGET 143 - Pray For Leaders And All Men

Bible Reading: 1st Timothy 2:1 -2
Therefore, I exhort first of all that supplications, prayers, intercessions, and giving of thanks be made for all men.
For kings and all who are in authority, so that we may lead a quiet and peaceful life in all godliness and honesty.

In 1st Timothy 2:1-2, Apostle Paul, a servant of God spoke of communication to our God through prayers and how it should be done. He advised us to live exemplary life of prayer through supplications by which we make our request known to God, through daily prayers by which we talk, relate and commune with our father daily and through intercession by which we pray for others including our relatives saved and unsaved for them to be saved. He also advised us to pray for even our enemies for them to repent and to cultivate the habit of giving thanks by which we thank God for all He has done for us which makes Him glorified and happy and ready to do even more for us.

Beloved, the scripture also told us that apart from praying for ourselves and others we should also pray for our leaders that they may govern well and that we may live in a peaceful environment. The importance of praying for those in authority cannot be overemphasized. If we neglect to pray for them, they will not lead well, there will be conflicts here and there in our lands, violence and all forms of crime and evils will abound and the preaching of the gospel of our Lord Jesus Christ will be inhibited and would not be spread as Christ directed.

Also people will not receive the gospel because their hearts are troubled and filled with anxieties.

Let us always remember that the responsibility to pray and communicate with God always is ours and not only for ourselves but for others, our lands, our leaders and for all men.

NUGGET 144 - Hide The Word Of God In Your Heart To Avoid Sin

Bible Reading: **Psalms** 119:11
Thy word have I hid in my heart, that I might not sin against thee.

Are you struggling with a particular sin? Is there any particular habit in your life that God does not approve of that you are finding hard to get rid of? Beloved, the word of God is what you need. The Psalmist said that the word of God had he hid in his heart so that he would not sin against God. God's word has the power to subdue sin in your heart. It is powerful, sharper than any two edged sword that pierces into the dividing asunder of marrows, joints, souls and spirits (Hebrews 4:12).

Those sinful thoughts that would not easily go away, the word of God in your heart can cut through them and bring them unto subjection. Those long term formed bad and sinful habits that have defiled all manner of prayers, the word of God can extinct them and bring them to abrupt end.

The word of God in your heart is your power over sin; just like it has the power to heal, it also has the power to deliver and set free from sin for where the word of a King is, there is power; power against sin (Ecclesiastes 8:4). It is the word of God that you have kept in your heart and remember that will actually keep you from sin when an opportunity to sin comes.

The issue is how much of the word do you know and how can you apply the word of God to deliver and keep you from sinning against God. You can achieve a sinless life easily by emulating the Psalmist, David. He hid the word of God which is the best thing, in the best place which is his heart and for the best purpose which is to avoid sinning against God.

Whomever you love, you try not to off end. David loved God and did not want to displease Him so he hid His word in the most treasured part of him, his heart, to remember it, to reverence it and to practice it. God's word is the best preventive measure against off ending God, for it tells us his mind and will, and tends to bring your spirit into conformity with His.

Beloved, there is no better place to keep the word of God than the heart for if you keep it in your mouth only, it can be taken away; if you record it in your book, the book might get missing but if you lay it up in your heart, as Mary did with the words of the angel (Luke 2:19), no enemy shall ever be able to take it away from you and that guides you to living a holy and acceptable life unto God.

NUGGET 145 - After That You Have Suffered A While

Bible Reading: 1st Peter 5:10
But the God of all grace, who hath called us unto His eternal glory by Christ Jesus, after that ye have suffered a while, make you perfect, establish, strengthen, settle you.

Beloved, suffering is not ruled out once you accept Christ as your Lord and saviour, any gospel that excludes suffering out of the Christian journey is not a true gospel. Therefore, sufferings, trials and temptations are inevitable in our Christian journey. Jesus in John 6:33 said that in the world we shall have tribulations. Jesus did not promise us a rosy road to heaven. He did not promise us rosy lives on earth either but the God of all grace who had called us unto His eternal glory by Christ Jesus confirmed through His word that though we shall experience suffering but the suffering is just for a while. Beloved, this means that the suffering is not permanent. It is not forever, it is only a transition. It is not a final destination; it is a passing through and it shall pass.

The scripture further said that the suffering has a purpose and that the reasons why we must suffer for a while are for us to be made perfect; for us to be established, for us to be strengthened and for us to be settled. You can see beloved that our God is not a wicked God that allows His own to suffer deliberately for all things work together for them that love Him. The suffering is just to make you better, stronger spiritually and more established in Him trusting Him more. The suffering is also to make you bigger and unshakable as He promised to settle you at the end of it all just like He did to Job.

NUGGET 146 - Give God Your Time

Bible Reading: **Ephesians 5:16**
Redeeming the time, because the days are evil.

Time they say waits for no body, the clock is ticking fast; eternity is fast approaching. As we start our journey into Christians stewardship, we start out by looking at how we should be good stewards of one of our most precious resources, our time. Despite how busy we may be, or make ourselves to be, God is asking for our times. Ephesians 5:16 enjoined us to make the most of our times because the days are evil.

Beloved there is a lot of work to be done; procrastination is very dangerous. The harvest is plentiful but the labourers are few. God is looking for those to work for Him. He is expecting us to spare some time for His work and giving Him our times for His work as much as we give to every other important things in our lives. Heaven and the kingdom business are about the most important things in our lives because we are just sojourners on earth and our destination is heaven.

Beloved, how much time out of your week do you give to God? How much time do you give to evangelism for a month? How much time do you spend studying God's word? How much time do you give to prayers not necessarily to ask for anything but just to worship, sing praises or make melodies in your hearts to God. Remember that whoever that gives time to God will not have time for the devil.

Endeavor to make time for God out of your busy schedules and while mapping out time for the activities for the day or for the week or for the month, also give God His own time because the benefits are numerous.

NUGGET 147 - Thou Shall Condemn

Bible Reading: **Isaiah 54:17**
No weapon that is formed against thee shall prosper and every tongue that shall rise againstthee in judgement thou shalt condemn. This is the heritage of the servants of the Lord and their righteousness is of me, saith the Lord.

This end time is associated with so much evil. The activities of the kingdom of darkness are on the increase but the good news is that God had provided tools with which to counter their attacks and secure victory and these tools are in His words. You can only discover, know and utilise these tools when you search and study God's words, the Bible.

Isaiah 54:17 is one of the tools to secure victory against the weapons of the enemy including evil tongues and voices no matter the weapon and no matter what the tongue is saying. The tongues could be what the doctor has said or what the 'over my dead body' enemies and powers of darkness have said but the word of God said that you shall condemn them all which means they shall speak and you shall condemn whatever you have. Do not give room for whatever they have spoken to stay, condemn immediately. You cannot stop them from speaking but you can stop their words from coming to pass.

Beloved, use Isaiah 54:17 to stop the tongue speaking sickness, failure, slow progress, backwardness, disappointment and all sorts of evil into your life and obtain victory even in this end time also remember that the conclusion of that scripture needs you to be a servant of God and in right standing with Him.

NUGGET 148 - God Is A Covenant Keeping God

Bible Reading: Ps 89:34
My covenant will I not break no alter the thing that is gone out of my lips.

Beloved, it is impossible for God to lie. He keeps His word and can never break His covenant with His children. Go through the whole scriptures and you will find out that there is no where God promised His people and failed. He only changes His ways and not His mind.

God promised the Israelites the land of Canaan and He eventually gave it to them. Has God promised you anything? What has He said He will do for you either through His word or through a word of prophecy? Is what He promised you taking too long, then Psalms 89:34 is for you, hold Him by that scripture. His promises are yea and amen in Christ. Anything God has said He will do He will do, He has exalted His words above His name. He is God of integrity and there is no variableness nor shadow of turning in with Him. He never forgets his word, He foresees all events, He is able to perform, He is true and faithful. Therefore whatever is gone out of his lips will never be altered but will most certainly be fulfilled; heaven and earth shall pass away but whatever that came out of His lips shall never pass away.

Beloved, when you understand the seriousness of how God takes His words, you will never worry again as to whether what He has promised you will come to pass or not. When Jesus, His only begotten son bled and died on the cross to give mankind salvation and eternal life, it was a promise fulfilled. When God said He had prepared a place called heaven for the believers, it was not a lie. People who have had encounters with death and were brought back to life confirmed that the Promise of heaven is sure. So beloved whether in the past, present or in the future, God promises are yea and Amen. All you have to do is to believe, trust and obey Him.

NUGGET 149 - Why Worry When You Can Pray

Bible Reading: **Mathew 6:31**
Therefore take no thought, saying, what shall we eat? or what shall we drink? or where withal shall we be clothed?

Beloved, excessive worry and anxiety leads to depression, frustration and elevated blood pressure but why worry while you are admonished by the scriptures to take no thought. Take no thought means do not think; do not worry. Another scriptures said be anxious for nothing but in whatever it is, pray, give thanks and tell it to God.

Beloved, have you ever prayed and prayed through and suddenly a feeling of calmness overwhelms you and you have peace in your heart? That is exactly what God wants from you whenever you have a worrisome situation at hand. He does not want you to worry because He knows what that will bring. He knows worry will bring you sickness, doubt and unbelief. So instead of worrying, give Him thanks because thanksgiving is key. Giving Him thanks instead means you trust Him. It involves remembering what He did when you were in similar situation and giving Him thanks for it and that makes you more confident that He will still what you asked of Him and that confidence kills worry.

A heart full of thanks can never be sad at the same time because as you are thanking Him, your heart is full of joy in anticipation of an answered prayer as if He has already done it and such heart challenges God and spurs Him to action. Therefore beloved, worry less and pray more for worry can never solve a problem but prayer can.

NUGGET 150 - The Father Hath Not Left Me Alone

Bible Reading: **John 8:29**
And He that sent me is with me, the father hath not left me alone; for I do always those things that please Him.

Beloved, has God given you a particular task or assignment? Has He called you to do His work? Has He called you to take up your cross and follow Him? Has He sent you to a particular place to do something? Has He sent you to a particular church or home to accomplish a task? What about the reason for which you are created; the reason for which you are born into a particular home? Has He sent you as a Moses to deliver a certain people? Has He sent you as a Jonah to preach and evangelise a people?.

Beloved, what is it that God has sent you to do? I want you to know that He is with you. He has not left you alone for whosoever He calls, He equips. He will never leave nor forsake you even if the road and the journey is tough. He will always be with you to help you accomplish that task or assignment only if you do what pleases Him and if you do not disobey His orders and directions just like Jesus did.

CHAPTER 16

Nugget 151
Two Cannot Walk Together Except They Agree To

Nugget 152
It Is A Prayer Thing Bible

Nugget 153
Be A Vessel Unto Honour

Nugget 154
If Jesus Has Set You Free, You Are Free Indeed

Nugget 155
For The Lord Thy God, He It Is That Doth Go With Thee

Nugget 156
Rebuke And Resist That Devil

Nugget 157
Do Not Allow The Enemy Steal Your Joy

Nugget 158
They Shall Be Strong And Do Exploits

Nugget 159
Follow After Righteousness

Nugget 160
Be Thou An Example

NUGGET 151 - Two Cannot Walk Together Except They Agree To

Bible Reading: Amos 3:3
Can Two walk together, except they be agreed?

Amos 3:3 described the power of agreement. It described that whatever or whoever you allow to follow you does so with your consent. Two cannot walk together except they be in agreement with each other. In other words, if one says no the other cannot follow in the walking.

Beloved, sickness is one and you are two, worry is one and you are two, so also sin, failure and unbelief. These things cannot come into your life, stay and accompany you around if you do not allow them. These things stay most times because we notice their early signs in the case of sicknesses, welcome them and give them room to grow by not exercising the power and authority God has given us over them. The scripture said "rebuke the devil and he will flee".

Beloved, please do not let that little headache mature into migraine. Do not let that worry and anxiety mature into depression. Do not let that little lack of money mature into bankruptcy. Do not let that little mistake mature into a big issue you cannot handle and do not let that sin become a habitual sin. Rebuke them immediately you notice them following you and they will stop because two cannot walk together accept there is an agreement between both parties.

NUGGET 152 - It Is A Prayer Thing

Bible Reading: **Mathew 17:21**
Howbeith this kind goeth out not but by prayer and fasting.

Beloved, there are situations and times we find ourselves in and we know that these are not about anything else but prayer. Jesus said in Mathew 17:21 that this type of situation does not need anything else but prayer and fasting.

When you go to the hospital and they could not diagnose anything and yet you are feeling symptoms just know that it not a hospital thing but a prayer thing. When such happens, leave them and go to the one who created your body, who knows all your body parts. He knows what is wrong and He knows just what to do, He will fix it.

Have you written exams several times and you cannot understand why you should not pass the exams because you had put in your best; just know that it is no more a read and pass thing, it is a prayer thing. Go to God and table the matter; He will remove every hinderance and obstacle and you will excel.

Are you working so hard and doing several jobs and you have tried so hard to save up money to buy a mortgage or start or finish up a project and you seem to be making no headway? Beloved, just know that it is a prayer time for you cannot do it just by that and by yourself. You need the one that gives you the power to make wealth. Go to Him in prayer and you will build that house with ease and your project will end well.

Are you in so much debt and as the days go by the debt is accumulating and you have tried to pay and the account is not balancing and always in red? It is time to give the matter to the one who paid a debt through the belly of a fish. He is a specialist in that area, He knows how best to get you out of that debt.

Beloved, whatever you have tried to achieve or accomplish or whatever you have tried to become and whatever you need and it is almost becoming impossible, just go to the rock that is higher than all, the one who makes the impossible possible and you will smile after all.

NUGGET 153 - Be A Vessel Unto Honour

Bible Reading: **2nd Timothy 2:21**
If a man therefore purge himself from these, he shall be a vessel unto honour, sanctified, and meet for the master's use, and prepared unto every good work.

A vessel is a container. A vessel is a carrier. A vessel is a conveyor. A vessel can be used for various purposes. What a vessel can convey depends on what it carries. A vessel carrying junks and rubbish can only convey junks and rubbish, a vessel carrying goodies can only convey goodies. That is why it is important we check what we carry; purge ourselves of junks and evil if we carry any with the blood of Jesus, with the word of God and the renewal of our minds so we can be fit for The Master's use.

God cannot use us as vessels if what we carry evil and what is contained inside of us is evil and sinful. There are vessels unto honour which bring honour and glory to the user (God) and there are vessels unto dishonour which bring dishonour, disrepute and shame to the user. God is interested in a purged and ready to be used containers.

Beloved, the scripture said that if any man purges himself, he will be a vessel unto honour which means that there must be a purging first before use. You cannot use a utensil in your house that is dirty without first of all washing off the dirt; so also God cannot use us for any good works except we purge ourselves from all dirtiness, fleshy desires, sins and all appearances of sins.

God is always ready to use us but how ready are we to be used. His eyes cannot behold iniquity and therefore will not waste time to depart from any vessel once it is tempered with by sin. Therefore beloved, let us therefore lay aside every sin that easily beset us so we can be that vessel unto honour that the Master can use and continue to use unto good works.

NUGGET 154 - If Jesus Has Set You Free, You Are Free Indeed

Bible Reading: **John 8:36**
If the Son therefore shall make you free, ye shall be free indeed.

The above scripture refers to the deliverance of man from sin and death. Jesus was the revelation of God's grace to all men. Freedom from sin, unrighteousness and death only comes from the cleansing by the blood of Jesus. This freedom also applies to freedom from oppression, sorrow, sicknesses, and powers of darkness and their evil works. This freedom comes from trusting God for justification not by good works. It is only when one comes to God through Jesus that he can be able to experience this true freedom.

Jesus has come to set us free from all entanglement of sin and all manner of oppressions and captivity. His death on the cross brought us this freedom and therefore if Jesus has set us free, we are free indeed.

Therefore beloved, walk with that confidence that your freedom has been paid for and secured by Christ Jesus. You are now no longer indebted to sin and you owe the devil nothing and he no longer have right to oppress or oppose you in any way and you have the right to walk in that liberty wherewith Christ Jesus has set you free to live for Him.

Beloved, if Jesus has already set you free, you are free regardless of what the devil brings your way, just believe it, act on it and it will work for you.

NUGGET 155 - For The Lord Thy God, He It Is That Doth Go With Thee

Bible Reading: Deut. 32:6
Be strong and of good courage, fear not, nor be afraid of them for the Lord thy God, He it is that doth go with thee; He will not fail thee, nor forsake thee.

Moses worked with God long enough to know whom He is. He had a very close relationship with God, he knew the capabilities of God because of the wonders He did during his walk with him. He knew God too much that if God says He will do something, for sure He will. If He said He is going to be with His people, He definitely will. That was why Moses confidently spoke to the Israelites saying "the Lord thy God, it is He that doth go with thee.

Beloved, please it is pertinent to note that Moses first of all told the Israelites be strong, to be of a good courage, to fear not and not to be afraid of the enemies.

For any promise of God to work for you or come to fulfillment in your life, you must activate it all by yourself (Hebrew 11:40) for the scripture said that the just shall live by his own faith (Habakkuk 2:4).

Therefore beloved, whatever it is you are engaged in, be it battles of life, battles against the enemies of your destiny, battles against your spiritual growth, battles against your calling and battles against your wellness and health; the lord thy God, He, it is that doth go with thee and you shall conquer all, only be strong, of a good courage and do not be afraid of the enemies not even their numbers, their increased activities or their potencies. Do not exercise any form of fear, have faith that He is surely with you through it all and watch Him answer His name 'Emmanuel' in those battles.

NUGGET 156 - Rebuke And Resist That Devil

Bible Reading: **James 4:7**
Submit yourselves therefore to God. Resist the devil and he will flee from you.

Beloved, temptations, trials, evil desires and the urge to drift away from Christ are unavoidable since we are still wearing our mortal bodies. We encounter temptations everywhere we go and anytime but the good news is that there is always a way out.

Jesus was tempted despite that He is God but He handled it and did not sin. Please notice that Jesus rebuked the devil and Peter saying "get thee behind me Satan" in Luke 4:8 and Mathew 16:23 respectively. Why would Jesus refer one of His trusted and dedicated disciple as satan? It is because satan has a possessing power; he can possess anybody and anything to discourage you and the work you are doing for God. It is therefore advised that you be spiritually alert to recognise that satan and deal with him immediately.

When temptation or an evil thought that could mature into sin if not checked comes, how do you handle it? Do you begin to dwell on the thought and nurture it until it becomes a full blown sin or do you rebuke the thought immediately and say like Jesus "get thee behind me satan". Beloved, it is better to rebuke and arrest that satan in that thought before it hatches into sin and immediately, that evil thought plus the devil behind it will flee. When that devil flees, the joy of the Lord will suddenly overwhelm you because you have conquered the devil. This applies to sicknesses and all other unpleasant situations that satan brings.

Beloved, please note that the scripture said in James 4:7 to submit yourself to God first then resist the devil and he will flee. The scripture said that we are not unmindful of the devices of the devil. If you submit yourself to God and His Holy Spirit, you will always know when it is satan at work then you rebuke and resist him and he will flee from you.

NUGGET 157 - Do Not Allow The Enemy Steal Your Joy

Bible Reading: 1st Thessalonians 5:16
Rejoice evermore

Beloved, if there is anything the devil desires so much, it is to steal your joy, to make you sad all the time, to see that you do not experience the joy the salvation of your soul gives and the joy your heavenly father gives. The reason the devil desires so much to steal your joy is because he knows that he is already doomed for life and that there is no more repentance for him so he wants you to share in his everlasting sadness and sorrow with him. Another reason he wants to steal your joy is that he knows that heaven is meant for you and it is full of joy; so he does not want you to start experiencing that joy from here before you get to heaven.

The devil is an expert in stealing the joy of the children of God. He does not want you to be happy and seeing that this is his agenda what do you do? Rejoice always!!! Even if the enemy is trying so hard to make it impossible, resist him and he will flee, he has no choice when you persist and resist him in the name of Jesus that is above every other name including his name.

Any situation he brings your way, take it to God and leave Him to handle it and then fill your heart with joy instead of sadness. His mission is to kill, steal and to destroy your joy but he cannot because God, your father is there too with a counter mission to love you, care for you and meet your needs and give you joy and in abundance.

Kingdom of God is righteousness, peace, joy evermore in the Holy Ghost. It is with joy that you can draw water from the wells of salvation (Isaiah 12:3). You cannot know Christ and always be sad, you can never carry Christ and carry an aura of unhappiness and sadness all the same time because the joy of the Lord is supposed to be your strength even when things are not okay. This is because you have hope that things will eventually get better, that God is in that situation with you and that hope gives you joy and keeps you moving on.

Beloved, let us start experiencing the joy of the Lord, not the joy that fat bank account gives nor the joy that earthly possessions gives but the joy that God gives, the joy that salvation gives, the joy that your name in the book of life gives, the joy that God knows your name, the joy that God is with you gives and the joy that God loves you so dearly gives. Do not ever let the devil steal that joy.

NUGGET 158 - They Shall Be Strong And Do Exploits

Bible Reading: Daniel 11:32
And as such that do wickedly against the covenant shall he corrupt by flatteries; but the people that do know their God shall be strong and do exploits.

In these days of so much happenings and perils, strength from knowing the Lord is required because it is not by mere human might but by the strength of the Lord shall we pull through. If we depend on our strength we will be battered and bruised in the ongoing battles between the kingdom of darkness and God's elects for by strength shall no mortal prevail over the kingdom of darkness.

We need God more than ever right now, we need to know Him more, search for Him and hold tenaciously onto Him so that when there is famine, we can enjoy plenty. When there is a casting down, we will be lifted. When there is low economy, we will flourish. Even when there is shadow of death around, we will walk through it fearing nothing. When enemies are plenty on every side, they will be used to prepare beautiful tables before us and in the midst of sorrow, we will laugh. In the event of outbreak of disease we will enjoy good and divine health. Even if the fig tree does not blossom now, we will not be bordered because we know that the fig tree will eventually blossom for we know the God we serve. We have a strong relationship with Him and because we have a strong relationship with Him, we have a strong backing from Him therefore we will do exploits.

NUGGET 159 - Follow After Righteousness

Bible Reading: 1 Timothy 6: 11
But thou O man of God, flee these things; and follow after righteousness, godliness, faith, love, patience, meekness.

Beloved, 1 Timothy 6:11 is advising us to seek first righteousness which will enable us be in favour with God and with men which in turn will give us breakthroughs in all areas of our lives. It also said we should live a godly life which will automatically command God's blessings upon our lives and clear all obstacles on our ways to greatness.

It is possible to be blinded by greed, even to the point of losing our faith but being faithful to God and having faith in Him remain the ways to get all we want in life. There is no other way. If we allow the love of money to get through to us, and we eventually make all the money in the world by the wrong means, we do not glorify God and such wealth and blessings bring nothing but sorrow and unfulfilled life with it. Such moves will not please God and God cannot behold unrighteousness.

Beloved, living our lives only focused on money brings sorrow. We are called to trust God, pursue righteousness and a godly life rather than pursuing earthly things. When our focus is first on Him, He is faithful to provide every other things we need according to His riches in glory.

NUGGET 160 - Be Thou An Example

Bible Reading: 1st Timothy 4:12
Let no man despise thy youth, but be thou an example to the believers, in word, in conversation, in charity, in spirit, in faith, in purity.

1st Timothy 4:12 is an injunction by Apostle Paul to us believers to live an exemplary life to other believers and to unbelievers as well. Let our words and our conversations be as such that someone would emulate. The way we love others, the way we love God, the way we serve God and the way we live our lives should all be worthy of emulation.

Beloved, let our light so shine before men that they may see our good works and glorify God. It is very important we be examples to others especially the younger generation and our children for the continuity of Christianity. If we do not live a life that the younger generations would emulate and continue, Christianity and Christian values might face out and God forbid that that should happen in our times.

Beloved, are you a pacesetter? Are you mentoring someone right now? Do people emulate you? Do they look up to you? Do young people look at your life and want to be like you? Do people approach you and say that they admire your courage and wishes to have the same grace as you do? It is very possible to be a role model, all it takes is hard work and putting God first in everything.

Let us strive to live that life worthy of emulation. Let us not be the reason why someone will fall out of faith. Let us not aid the devil to depopulate heaven by the kind of life we live rather let us be light and let our light lead those in darkness to the right way that leads to heaven.

CHAPTER 17

Nugget 161
Invite Jesus

Nugget 162
Humility

Nugget 163
Do Unto Others What You Wish Them Do Unto You

Nugget 164
Do Not Miss Your Old Ways Of Life

Nugget 165
Have Compassion For Souls

Nugget 166
He Is Faithful And Just To Forgive

Nugget 167
He Prepares A Table Even In The Midst Of Enemies

Nugget 168
Honour Thy Father And Thy Mother

Nugget 169
Jesus Heals Every Sickness And Every Disease

Nugget 170
You Are A Chosen Generation

NUGGET 161 - Invite Jesus

Bible Reading: Mark 6:3
Is not this the carpenter, the son of Mary, the brother of James, and Joses, and of Juda, and Simon? and are not His sisters here with us? And they were offended at Him.

Beloved, have you ever been to a Capenter's workshop? What did you see? Am sure you saw some raw materials as well as unfinished products still at their skeletal stages. And I bet you if you visit that same workshop in few weeks time you will see those raw materials turned into finished products and those same unfinished ugly looking products at their skeletal stages turned into very beautiful, attractive and costly sofas. Most of us when we pass through the Capenter's shop and see him working at the skeletal stages, we wonder what he could be making and only when he finishes we now understand and see what he has made. As the wood goes through so many cuttings, shaping, reshaping and polishing before it turns out beautiful so do we when we are 'in the making' by Jesus, our Capenter. Jesus can allow you pass through so many hurdles, difficulties, trials just to make you. There are some situations He brings your way just to perfect you and make you a beautiful soul lacking nothing spiritually and physically.

Beloved, be patient when the Lord Jesus, The Capenter is making you so you do not run faster than your shadows and miss that beautiful end He had planned for you. The Capenter mends things too so invite Jesus into your home, your business, your career, your job if they need mending and He will mend all.

NUGGET 162 - Humility

Bible Reading: **Proverbs 22:4**
By humility and fear of the Lord are riches, and honour, and life.

Beloved, humility is a virtue, it is the opposite of pride and the scriptures in James 4:6 said that God resists the proud and gives grace to the humble. Pride made the devil who was a gifted Angel of God to loose his place and now is doomed forever. God hates pride and resist whoever that exhibits pride and could hate such a person and it is a very dangerous situation to be in. It means God will oppose anything the person has, does or wants to do. He will refrain the person and the person will not receive anything from Him. On the other hand, the humble is given grace; grace to be rich, grace to prosper more and grace to live long enough to enjoy the riches and afterwards, eternal life.

Beloved, one can only enjoy riches, honour, life and all other things that life off ers by submission to the will of God, by fear of God and by humility. Let us emulate the humility of Christ and it shall be well with us.

NUGGET 163 - Do Unto Others What You Wish Them Do Unto You

Bible Reading: **Mathew 7:12**
Therefore all things whatsoever ye would that men should do to you, do ye even so to them: for this is the law and the prophet.

Beloved, every action will be accounted for on the last day when we shall stand before the judgement throne of God which is why we should strive to right our actions here on earth.

Mathew 7:12 is our Lord Jesus Christ's injunction to us today which is often referred to as 'The Golden Rule'. This simply means we should always be considerate; we should not hurt others when we know that we would not like it when we are hurt in same way. We should not maltreat others when we know that if same treatment were given to us we would not appreciate it. We should not judge others wrongly when we know that it will not go down well with us when same is done to us. We should not scheme to bring others down when we know that we would not take it if same is done to us.

Beloved, it is all about the principle of loving our neighbours as ourselves. If we love ourselves we would not kill ourselves, we would not cheat ourselves and we will always look after ourselves. God expects us to love others just same way we love ourselves. Mathew 7:12 is a fundamental principle of Christian life that manifests one's relationship both with his fellow Christians as well as non Christians alike. It is not a selfish motivation for being kind to others but a mental check by which we can continually guard our behaviours in relation to others. The actions and life of our Lord Jesus Christ when He was on earth demonstrated a perfect example of such. Beloved, let us therefore emulate Him and the world will be a better place for us all to dwell in.

NUGGET 164 - Do Not Miss Your Old Ways Of Life

Bible Reading: **2nd Corinthians 5:17**
Therefore If any man be in Christ, he is s new creature: old things are passed away; behold, all things are become new.

2nd Corinthians 5:17 simply means that if anyone accepts Christ as his Lord and Saviour, he is no longer the old person he used to be because there must be a noticeable difference between him now and him before. All the evil ways are completely forgotten and gone, taken away by the blood of Jesus and everything at the moment is totally new, good and pleasing unto God. Also the person cannot wish to go back to his old ways.

Beloved, one way to bit addiction is total abstinence so also a habitual sin or old ways; the scripture said flee from them which means take to your heels or run away from them. It is a wonder when a spirit filled, tongue talking, born again Christian hails people indulging in the old ways such Christian Left behind when he got born again instead of having pity on their souls and praying for God to deliver them. It is also a wonder when a believer utters words like "how I wish it was when I was in the world, I would have dealt with you". Beloved, would Jesus have uttered such words? Jesus would have said " father forgive them for they know not what they do". Some profess Christ and when no one is looking, they magnify the devil and his works. Beloved it ought not to be so. Let us emulate our Lord Jesus Christ, He was what He said He was anytime, any day, everywhere during His earthly mission even till death and in heaven now He is still the righteous lamb of God.

The devil has deceived some Christians into going back to their old ways because they could not cope with living the life of Christ because to them it is hard and the old ways seem more enjoyable. Beloved, that is the trick of the devil. To live for Christ is gain because of the eternal life attached to it and with the help of the Holy Spirit it is quite easy. The only task is to ask for the Holy Spirit, listen and obey when He guides and gradually those old ways will look stupid, undesirable and a no no. God will help us.

NUGGET 165 - Have Compassion For Souls

Bible Reading: **Mathew 9:35**
And Jesus went about all the cities and villages, teaching in their synagogues and preaching the gospel of the kingdom and healing every sickness and every disease among the people.

Jesus went about the cities teaching and preaching the gospel of the kingdom. We too as His followers should follow His footsteps of teaching and preaching the gospel to others to save their souls for this is one of His commandments. Jesus was sympathetic for the physical needs of people as well as their spiritual needs because He knew that it is not the wish of His father for any to perish but for all to come to repentance. Most of His healing of the sick and preaching of the gospel were motivated by His compassion for souls.

Nowadays, devil has occupied the minds of most believers with issues of life so much that they forget about the needful which is the preaching of the gospel. It is the agenda of the devil to make Christians forget preaching the gospel. Christians should not allow such plans by the devil, the hater of gospel and the children of God.

Beloved, sometimes we do not nee too much prayer for our problems to receive solutions but by simple act of doing something for God, reaching out to the unsaved souls and the needy in the society. Let us therefore even in our busiest schedules, make out time for Evangelism even if it is the sharing of Christian leaflets with messages of salvation. Even if you cannot go out to preach, you can pray in your closets for souls to be saved sending out the

Holy Spirit of God to do His work of convincing and converting sinners unto repentance. We can also give our money to be used for the propagation of the gospel, that too would be counted for us by God.

NUGGET 166 - He Is Faithful And Just To Forgive

Bible Reading: 1st John 1:9
If we confess our sins, He is faithful and just to forgive us our sins, and to cleanse us from all unrighteousness.

Beloved, are you still carrying the weight of sin and the guilt thereof? Are you thinking in your mind that that sin is too heavy for God to forgive? Has the devil robbed you of your confidence because of that sin? Has the devil said to you that you have no right to come before the presence of your maker?

Isaiah 1:18 enjoined you to go reason together with your God, even if your sin is as scarlet it shall be made white as snow. So lay it down with the simple act of confessing to God. He is ever faithful and just. He will wash away the stains of that sin, leaving you as white as snow so you can go boldly to His presence to obtain everything you need. But try as much as you can not to continue in that sin, ask the Holy Spirit to help you and He will.

NUGGET 167 - He Prepares A Table Even In The Midst Of Enemies

Bible Reading: **Ps 23:5**
Thou preparest a table before me in the presence of mine enemies, thou anointest my head with oil, my cup runneth over.

God our Heavenly Father knows that enemies are inevitable, in fact they are most times used by Him to bring us closer and make us come running to Him. He also uses our enemies as tools to bring us to our place of destiny. Enemies are part of our journeys in life. Even God Himself has enemies. Jesus during His sojourn on earth had several enemies even though He never sinned nor wronged anyone.

Beloved, if you do not have enemies you really need to check if God has deposited some good things in you because it is only a tree with good fruits that attracts pluckers. If you have something good in you, the enemies must abound but the good news is that even in the midst of these enemies God will prepare a table before you but you have to please Him first by obeying His commands and following His precepts.

David had enemies but because he was a man after God's own heart God prepared a table before him even in the presence of those enemies. So also beloved if you please God, He will prosper you even in the midst of the attacks of the enemies here and there.

Strive therefore to please God and He will take care of your enemies and prosper you even in their midst.

NUGGET 168 - Honour Thy Father And Thy Mother

Bible Reading: Exodus 20:12
Honour thy father and thy mother; that thy days may be long upon the land which the Lord thy God giveth thee.

One of the things among other factors that will qualify us for long life is honouring our parents, whether as children or as adults. Long life is one of the promises of God to His children and it has pre requisition attached to it. Honouring our parents involve taking care of them especially when they are old, obeying their good instructions and living in a way that will not make them lament to God over us. Even if they are no more, we are still supposed to keep honouring them by taking care of the seeds they left behind and making sure we live good lives as if they were still alive in order to obtain longevity.

Beloved, honouring our parents indirectly honours God and honouring God indirectly honours our parents. So let us start by showing them great love in anyway we can; do not ever forget them because there is long life in taking care of them.

NUGGET 169 - Jesus Heals Every Sickness And Every Disease

Bible Reading: **Mathew 9:35**
And Jesus went about all the cities and villages teaching in their synagogues and preaching the gospel of the kingdom and healing every sickness and every disease among the people.

Jesus is ever the same, as He was yesterday so He is today and so shall He be forever; He never changes. He did heal in His days, He is still that same Jesus today; He is still healing people today and He can heal you.

Jesus healed every manner of sickness and disease even now there is no type of sickness and disease He cannot heal. Every sickness is included in the stripes He received on the way to the cross for by His stripes we are healed. He can heal whatever sickness it is including the ones in our bodies, the ones in our souls and the ones in our businesses.

The word of God said that greater works Jesus did, we will do. Beloved, you have the power to heal the sick too only if you have the faith; just command that sickness to go and it will go. Try it with faith reminding God of His words concerning healing and that healing will manifest.

NUGGET 170 - You Are A Chosen Generation

Bible Reading: 1st Peter 2:9
But ye are a chosen generation, a royal priesthood, an holy nation, a peculiar people; that ye should shew forth the praises of Him who hath called you out of darkness into His marvellous light.

Beloved, from the day you accepted Jesus as your Lord and became born again, you are no longer your own, you belong to Christ. You have become special, unique and redeemed. You should no longer carry the mentality of a no body and if you have not started seeing yourself as someone unique, you should change that mentality right away.

The scriptures said that you are a chosen person which means that you are a set aside, a touch not and only meant for special purposes. You are a rare being and a no ordinary person. The scripture went further to say that you are a royalty, a prince, a princess, a king who is clothed with beauty and glory; a king whose words carry power and authority. That is why when you decree a thing, it is established. When you speak, the devils obey and when you bind on earth, it is bound in heaven.

You are also a holy and a righteous person because the blood of your saviour Lord Jesus Christ cleanses you from every sin and unrighteousness and you are to live in that consciousness that you are no longer a slave to sin and walk in the righteousness of God. Therefore beloved, knowing that you are now a special being that has all the attributes listed in the scriptures, you should stop seeing yourself as anything less than what the scriptures said that you are. Stop limiting yourself and start being who God says you are.

www.ingramcontent.com/pod-product-compliance
Lightning Source LLC
Chambersburg PA
CBHW071557080526
44588CB00010B/935